Regulating European Labour Markets:
More Costs Than Benefits?

John T. Addison

University of South Carolina

and

W. Stanley Siebert

University of Birmingham

Published by The Institute of Economic Affairs
1999

First published in February 1999 by
The Institute of Economic Affairs
2 Lord North Street
Westminster
London SW1P 3LB

Hobart Paper 138
ISSN 0073-2818
ISBN 0-255 36420-2

Printed in Great Britain by
Hartington Fine Arts Limited, Lancing, West Sussex
Set in Baskerville Roman 11 on 12 point

Contents

Foreword

Intervention in employment contracts is a tempting field for politicians. Setting minimum wages and specifying other conditions of employment (such as annual holidays, parental leave and terms of dismissal) are obvious fields for political action because they appear to be direct means of improving the lot of workers. They are usually welcomed by trades unions, as representatives of those with jobs, and perhaps also by large companies which realise that such regulation hampers smaller competitors. But such actions have consequences, one of which may be to reduce employment below what it would otherwise be, not only because some existing workers lose their jobs but because some of the unemployed are prevented from moving into work.

The European Union has for many years been involved in action intended to improve working conditions, most notably via the 'social charter' and its predecessors from 1974 onwards. In Hobart Paper 138, Professors John Addison and Stanley Siebert – both internationally known for their work in the economics of labour markets – analyse some of the likely effects of what they describe as 'unalloyed labour market re-regulation' (page 34) in the EU.

They begin (Section II) with a history of how the European Commission has pursued social legislation, despite the '…very narrow treaty basis' it originally had. They trace the history of British opposition to such measures from Mrs Thatcher's veto, to the proposed social chapter of the Maastricht Treaty (from which Britain opted out), to the eventual acceptance of the chapter by the present government early in its term of office. The 1997 Treaty of Amsterdam incorporates the provisions of the earlier Agreement on Social Policy so it is now part of the European Union Treaties. Moreover, the Amsterdam Treaty includes an 'employment chapter' which '…opens up scope for considerable Commission activism in the future'.(page 25)

After surveying the status of Commission initiatives in the social field, Addison and Siebert turn (Section III) to the theory underlying the setting of minimum labour standards which relies essentially on market failure arguments (such as the presence of monopsony, externalities related to training and workplace safety and worker misinformation) and on equity considerations. They point out the presence of such failures does not in itself justify government or supranational action for it '...cannot be presumed that the government can be relied upon to correct matters'.

Empirical evidence should therefore be examined to determine what have been the effects, in practice, of labour market regulation. Addison and Siebert show (Section IV) there is a *prima facie* case that the less regulated economies (the United States, Japan and the United Kingdom) have been better generators of employment than the more regulated states of the EU. After examining various studies of the effects of employment protection and similar rules, they conclude that the

> '...net effect...does seem to be lower employment, greater and longer unemployment for some, and, implicitly, a decline in the speed with which labour relocates from declining to growing sectors of the economy.' (page 74)

The authors conclude (Section V) that, though the Commission has managed to have most of its social policy agenda enacted into law, it has failed to meet its obligation to evaluate the effects of its measures on the labour market. Indeed, they charge the Commission with 'sheer amateurishness' and basing its policies on 'ethereal notions of fundamental social rights'. Procedures in Brussels need to be reformed. In their view, an independent efficiency audit of social proposals is required so that the 'disemployment and other consequences' of new mandates can be independently investigated. The effects may be greater in Britain than elsewhere, given its different traditions.

This meticulous and lucid analysis by Professors Addison and Siebert presents a serious challenge to those who wish to carry forward an EU social programme on the simple presumption that it is bound to do good and who fail to investigate in detail its likely effects. After their paper, it should no longer be possible for reasonable people to pursue such an unprofessional approach.

All IEA papers contain the views of their authors, not those of the Institute (which has no corporate view), its Trustees, Advisers or Directors. But, in publishing Hobart Paper 138, the

6

Institute hopes to stimulate a more informed debate about the costs and benefits of social programmes in Europe.

January 1999   COLIN ROBINSON
Editorial Director, The Institute of Economic Affairs
Professor of Economics, University of Surrey

The Authors

JOHN T. ADDISON is Professor of Economics, and Business Partnership Distinguished Foundation Fellow at the University of South Carolina in the United States. He was educated at the London School of Economics (BSc, MSc, and PhD), where he specialised in labour economics. He has published widely in the major economics and specialist labour journals, including the *Journal of Business, American Economic Review, Review of Economics and Statistics*, and the *Journal of Labor Economics*. He is the author/editor of a number of labour economics texts, including *Labour Markets in Europe – Issues of Harmonization and Regulation* (London and New York: The Dryden Press/Harcourt Brace, 1997), co-edited with W. Stanley Siebert. In addition to work on the European Union, his research interests include the economics of trade unions, minimum wages, unemployment duration analysis, worker participation and firm performance, and the evaluation of mandates.

W. STANLEY SIEBERT is Professor of Labour Economics at the University of Birmingham. He was educated at the University of Cape Town and the London School of Economics, where he obtained MSc and PhD degrees. He is co-author, with Solomon W. Polachek, of *The Economics of Earnings* (Cambridge: Cambridge University Press, 1993). He has lectured widely in the United States, most recently as Visiting Professor at the University of Wisconsin – Milwaukee (from 1997). His research interests include the economics of discrimination, workplace health and safety, and the economics of education. For the IEA he has contributed 'The Market Regulation of Industrial Safety' to *Regulators in the Market* (IEA Readings No. 35, 1991), and, with John T. Addison, *Social Engineering in the European Community: the Social Charter, Maastricht and Beyond* (Current Controversies No. 6, 1993).

Acknowledgements

We are grateful for comments from Clive Belfield and two anonymous referees, but remain responsible for any errors. Addison also wishes to acknowledge research support from the John M. Olin Institute for Employment Practice and Policy at George Mason University.

J.T.A.
W.S.S.

I. Introduction

The United Kingdom has now signed on to the 'social chapter' and to all intents and purposes a two-track social Europe is now behind us. With the formal conclusion of the Treaty of Amsterdam on 2 October 1997, the 'social chapter' has at last become formally that, no longer consigned to a Protocol attached to the (Maastricht) treaty but now an integral part of the treaties establishing the European Union.[1]

What difference will the UK's opt-in make to the development of pan-European labour market rules? More generally, what is the logic of labour market regulation at European level? Are such rules a prerequisite of economic integration – or some type of social counterbalance to the competitive impulses imparted by economic and monetary union? And if they are not either of these, might they nevertheless be justified on equity grounds – or otherwise prove benign? These are among the issues examined in this monograph.

Arguably, the New Labour government would incline to the view that adherence to a European-wide social policy is something of a side-show; not terribly costly in terms of (British) jobs, while politically attractive in that it allows lip service to be paid to at least one element of Old Labour doctrine. Our interpretation on the costs side is rather different. Yet the more general position taken in this monograph is that the consequences *for Europe* of Britain's *volte face* amount to rather less than meets the eye. After all, Europe already had a substantive body of labour market regulation in place, plus the constituencies and the capability to pursue an active reform agenda with or without the UK. The British opt-in simply settles, once and for all, the competence or constitutional authority issue. But the opt-in

---

[1] The full text of the Treaty of Amsterdam is to be found on the web at http://ue.eu.int/Amsterdam/en/treaty/treaty.htm. The text of the earlier Maastricht Treaty is located at http://www.europa.eu.int/abc/obj/treaties/en/entoc01.htm.

does mean that other member states will now be able to seek relief from 'unfair competition' from one of their number. For this reason, the consequences for the UK in particular could be profound.

On the issue of labour market regulation, we take the position that each and every proposed Euro-mandate must be examined on its individual merits. Blanket rejection is inappropriate both intellectually and strategically. But each piece of draft legislation should be subject to a cost audit by a body other than the directorate-general for employment, industrial relations, and social affairs (DG-V), the agency responsible for framing social policy. This recommendation is important precisely because European social policy to date has been pursued largely as an article of faith, across-the-board and in a near analytical vacuum. Indeed, it is now almost politically incorrect to criticise social policy because such criticisms are seen to detract from the fundamental social rights of workers, which, post Amsterdam, are laid down as one of the general guiding principles of European Union.

To present our case, we *first* trace the long and chequered history of supranational labour market regulation in the European Union.[2] *Second*, we evaluate the broad rationale for social policy measures, on the basis of both orthodox economic analysis and the arguments used by the Commission. *Third*, although it is still too soon to chart the impact of Community labour market regulation, given the vintage of most of the measures and their patchy implementation by the member states,[3] we offer some empirical evidence on the effects of analogous mandates. *Finally*, we draw together the threads of the preceding analysis and amplify our policy conclusion.

---

[2] There is some unavoidable overlap between this part of the Paper and our previous IEA contribution (Addison and Siebert, 1993), even if our emphasis here is upon post-1993 developments.

[3] Witness the infringement proceedings currently being brought by the Commission against nearly all member states for failing to transpose into national law the 1994 directive on the protection of young people at work, on which more below.

II. From Social Action Plan Through Social Charter to Social Chapter

In the Beginning ...

The 'social chapter' which now anchors the social policy of the European Union can be traced back to 1974 – even earlier in the case of the more fundamental worker participation initiatives (see below) – when the Commission put forward a Social Action Plan (Commission, 1974). The Action Plan proposed mandates in areas such as health and safety at work, minimum wages, working hours, employee participation, and the hiring of contract labour.

The problem for the Commission – throughout we are referring specifically to DG-V – was that it had a very narrow treaty basis for pursuing social legislation, while yet having to pay due regard to the principle of 'subsidiarity' (the doctrine that Community action should only be envisaged where the set objective could be better secured at Community level than at national, member-state level.) By treaty basis, we mean those sections of the treaty establishing the common market (namely, the Treaty of Rome) that specifically deal with social policy. As a matter of fact, apart from establishing the principle of equal pay for equal work, the 1957 Treaty contained rather little having to do with social policy, its thrust being predominantly economic. That being said, the seeds of an embryonic Community social policy commitment are discernible in the Rome treaty.[4]

---

[4] In the Preamble to the Treaty of Rome, a 'constant improvement in living and working conditions' is stated as a central objective. This improvement was to be realised primarily through the liberalisation of trade and via economic mobility, rather than *ex ante* by means of social legislation. Nevertheless, Article 117 makes reference to the contribution of 'the approximation of legislative and administrative provisions' to this improvement, while Article 118 states that the Commission will seek to promote close co-operation between member states in the 'social field', covering among other things such matters as labour legislation and working conditions, social security, health and safety, employment, and collective bargaining.

13

Undeterred, the Commission proceeded on a number of fronts pursuant to its 1974 social action plan. It achieved some success in the area of health and safety regulation, where member states were apparently anxious not to be seen as competing and where it soon became accepted that the objective was not to be 'subordinated to purely economic considerations', and in its gender equality proposals. It also secured legislation offering workers protection in the event of collective redundancies, transfers of undertakings, and the insolvency of their employer. Unlike the health and safety regulations and gender directives, however, these employment protection laws arguably did little more than codify what was existing national practice.

Whenever the Commission strayed too far from national practice, however, it came up against the constraint that its measures had to be passed by unanimity in the 12-member Council of Ministers, the Community's decision-making agency. At that time, any member state could block social legislation by opposing it in Council. Although from 1979 on Mrs Thatcher came to be associated with use of this veto power, it is widely accepted that a number of nations hid behind her actions, while nonetheless expressing support for social legislation. In this way, they were able to appeal to opposing constituencies back home, thereby maximising electoral support. One indication of this is provided by Mrs Thatcher's success, albeit very short-lived, in securing what appeared to be a major redirection of Community policy in favour of flexibility in 1986 (Teague, 1989).

A number of important Commission initiatives fell foul of the unanimity rule. In the area of worker participation, they comprised the so-called 'Vredeling initiative', the European Company Statute (ECS), and the draft Fifth Directive on company law. The Vredeling proposal (first introduced in 1980 and amended in 1983) called for employees of multinational corporations to be given regular information on a wide range of economic, financial, business, and employment issues plus consultation on decisions likely to affect their interests. The two other proposals went much further. The ECS (first introduced in 1970 and amended in 1975) provided for worker representation on the supervisory board of any company that elected to become a European Company and thereby take advantage of a unified legal system

14

and certain interim tax advantages. It also required European Works Councils in such companies, much on the German pattern. The draft Fifth Directive for its part also proposed obligatory worker directors on the supervisory boards of all public corporations which employed 500 or more employees. Both pieces of draft legislation were amended by the Commission in the 1980s to take account of the absence of supervisory boards in a number of member states, including Britain, and also to allow for a wider range of participation options than board representation, but they still remained stalled in Council.

The Commission also was unable to secure legislation regulating part-time work. Its 1982/1983 proposals seeking equal treatment of part-timers with their full-time counterparts stumbled when confronted with the very real diversity of practice across member states, and trenchant British opposition. Similarly, the Commission's 1982 attempt to introduce licensing curbs on the operation of temporary employment agencies and to circumscribe the use of fixed-term contracts, as well as its 1983/1984 proposals seeking to establish a minimum of three months' parental leave and leave for family reasons, were also deadlocked in Council.

Mrs Thatcher's opposition to the Brussels bureaucracy was not of course simply visceral. It had a basis in pronounced system differences between Britain and her continental European neighbours (for example, the voluntaristic tradition in industrial relations) and what is commonly accepted to have been an over-mighty union movement. Moreover, in seeking root-and-branch reform of Britain's socialised economy, and its union movement, it was utterly logical for her to resist more labour market regulation.

But the *status quo* was shortly to change. In the first place, in an attempt to facilitate completion of the internal market, Mrs Thatcher acquiesced in an extension of majority voting under the Single European Act (SEA) of 1986, ratified the following year. This change would speed up decision-making and the achievement of economic union, but by the same token also make it easier to pass social legislation by undercutting a British veto. In the specific context of social policy, Mrs Thatcher may have thought that since the SEA strictly only provided for majority voting in matters of health and safety legislation (under Article 118A of the SEA),[5] this would minimise the danger. After all, the thrust of the SEA like that of its predecessor remained distinctly economic. Apart from Article 118A, it again contained little overt social policy content. Secondly, the entry of Spain and Portugal into the Community in 1986 changed attitudes on the part of other member states because the new entrants (plus Greece, which had been a member since 1981) raised the spectre of 'social dumping' or unfair competition (on which more below). A final factor was an improvement in economic conditions. Economic growth, if sustained, does of course take the edge off mandates that bite when the course of demand is uncertain. Even if it had once seemed that the Community was about to head down a deregulatory labour market path as a result of Mrs Thatcher's efforts, the stage was now set for a sea-change in matters of social policy.

The Social Charter

Only two years after the implementation of the SEA, the Community issued a solemn proclamation of fundamental social rights, the so-called 'social charter' of December 1989 (Commission, 1989a). The social charter was a declaratory statement that was not binding on its signatories – and Mrs Thatcher duly refused to endorse it – but it was accompanied by a detailed Social Action Programme, which contained no less than 47 separate initiatives, some 23 of which were to be the subject of binding legislation (Commission, 1989b). Each piece of draft legislation was to be brought before the (then) 12-member Council, despite Mrs Thatcher's refusal to endorse the social charter. On this occasion, if not subsequently, the UK was not to be excluded.

Legislative proposals came thick and fast in the wake of the publication of the social charter's action programme. The hallmark of the legislation was the Commission's creative use of a health and safety criterion under Article 118A. Examples include the proposed directives on the 48-hour maximum

---

[5] Article 118A of the SEA provides that 'Member States shall pay particular attention to encouraging improvements, especially in the working environment, as regards the health and safety of workers and shall set as their objective the harmonization of conditions in this area, while maintaining the improvements made'.

working week, pregnant workers, and child labour. These measures proved controversial precisely because they contained terms that had no well-determined link with health and safety and, insofar as they pertained to 'the rights and interests of employed persons', seemed to be directly undercut by another provision of the treaties establishing the common market, namely, Article 100A(2) which required unanimity. Meantime, Mrs Thatcher had been removed from office in November 1990.

Table 1 provides a thumb-nail sketch of the principal social charter directives or binding instruments. The order of the initiatives is broadly in ascending degree of controversiality, although this is inevitably a matter of judgement. Nevertheless, there can be little controversy over the measure updating the European system for the clearing of vacancies and applications (see the second element of item 1), and we have already alluded to the lack of political controversy attaching to the health and safety proposals (item 2). Equally, the measures stalled in Council at this time are self-evidently the most controversial (items 10 and 11).[6]

Progress on some of the more controversial of the measures identified in Table 1 cannot be considered in isolation from the next major institutional development in the form of the so-called 'social chapter'. By way of introduction, we note that in processing the measures detailed in the social action programme, whether under majority voting or unanimity, the Commission had to 'negotiate', watering down its proposals when it faced especial resistance in Council, typically spearheaded by the British.

Where unanimity was required, of course, British opposition necessarily meant that major social charter (and other initiatives)[7] were blocked. In particular, the Commission's atypical worker draft directives and a proposal seeking to establish works councils in European-level (that is, multi-national) corporations were in effect vetoed.

---

[6] Flesh is added to the skeletal framework of the entries in Table 1 by Addison and Siebert (1997, Table 2.1). And for information on the plethora of non-binding Community instruments foreshadowed in the social action programme, again see Addison and Siebert (1997, Table 2.2).

[7] The principal 'other' measures were the European Company Statute (and its sister draft directives covering European associations, co-operative societies, and mutual societies) and the Fifth Directive on Company Law.

Table 1: The Social Charter Initiatives in Ascending Order of Controversy

1. Modifications to existing Community vocational training programmes (OJ L214 of 2.8.91) and employment information systems (OJ L245 of 26.8.92).
2. Eleven health and safety initiatives, the bulk of which are rooted in the pre-social charter 1989 workplace health and safety framework directive 89/391/EEC(OJ L160 of 26.6.90). All but two of the initiatives have been enacted into law, final action being awaited on a measure dealing with risks arising from exposure to physical agents at work, while a proposal setting minimum health and safety standards in transport activities is now dormant.
3. Health and safety for atypical workers. Agency and fixed-term contract workers to be informed of job risks and to be trained accordingly. Health authorities to be notified of their deployment (OJ L206 of 29.7.92).
4. Modifications to existing Community law on collective redundancies. Main changes are *de facto* widening of the definition of the employee and augmented information and consultation rights (OJ L245 of 26.8.92).
5. Written contracts of employment to be provided to workers detailing the employment relation. Workers also to be given the name of the body determining the collective agreement (OJ L288 of 18.10.91).
6. Ban on child labour (except closely regulated 'light work'). Limitations also placed on the working hours of adolescents, prohibition of night work, and detailed health and safety requirements (OJ L216 of 20.8.94).
7. Workers 'posted' to another country to receive host country terms and conditions (OJ L18 of 21.1.97).
8. Regulation of the employment of pregnant workers. Such workers are to receive 14 weeks of maternity pay, to be remunerated at a level not less than the worker would have received if absent from work by reason of sickness. Eligibility requirements at member-state level not to exceed 12 months' service. Employers to provide risk assessment. Absolute ban on working with specific list of agents, processes, and working conditions. General ban on night work (OJ L348 of 28.11.92).
9. Regulation of working hours. Law fixes a maximum working week of 48 hours, although individuals can contract out (subject to Community review in seven years) and certain derogations apply in respect of the

reference period over which the 48-hour week is calculated. In addition, the law sets daily and weekly rest periods plus a three-week holiday entitlement. Normal hours of night workers are also regulated and such workers are to be given health assessments prior to job assignments and regularly thereafter (OJ L307 of 13.12.93). The UK abstained in the vote in Council, stating that it would challenge the legal basis (Article 118A) of the directive. The European Court of Justice dismissed the UK's submission on 12 November 1996, forcing implementation by 23 November 1996.

10. Two atypical worker directives subsequently consolidated into a single proposal. Original directives sought to regulate atypical work because of the 'increasing prevalence of insecurity and segmentation in the labour market' and 'distortions of competition'. Proposal(s) sought to give atypical workers comparable employment conditions to full-timers. These conditions included protection under statutory and occupational social security schemes, as well as holidays, vocational training, dismissal protection, and seniority allowances. Proposal withdrawn in December 1996 and processed under Agreement on Social Policy. (See Table 2.)

11. Establishment of European Works Councils with detailed information and consultation rights (OJ C336 of 31.12.91). As with item 10, the proposal was withdrawn and processed under Agreement on Social Policy. (See Table 2.)

The Commission would undoubtedly emphasise the compromises introduced into the social charter measures listed in Table 1 during the legislative process.[8] Thus, the Commission's draft proposal on collective redundancies (item 4) had initially called for such dismissals to be declared null and void in the event that the directive's information and consultation requirements had been breached by the employer side. This clause had to be dropped to secure adoption of the measure in Council. Similarly, the pregnant

---

[8] The situation is that the Commission proposes and the Council of Ministers disposes (i.e. legislates). The legislative process involves the European Parliament and has become increasingly more complicated through time as a result of new powers being ceded, the latter under revisions of the treaties establishing the common market. Today there are four possible legislative routes according to the particular treaty basis of draft proposals. These are the so-called 'consultation', 'co-operation', and 'co-decision' procedures – in ascending order of the Parliament's influence – plus a new route first opened up by the Agreement on Social Policy (see below).

workers directive (item 8) had originally called for maternity leave to be paid at 100 per cent of normal earnings, a provision which had to be trimmed back to a level consistent with the levels of sick pay obtaining in the individual member states. Again, the working time directive (item 9) had sought an inalienable 48-hour week, which was subsequently modified to allow workers to refuse to work more than this limit without penalty.

But compromise is a two-way process. In each of the above cases the proposals were also in part strengthened.[9] Indeed, it might reasonably be claimed that the Commission had by 1991 made very good progress on its many social charter initiatives. But the Commission continued to be frustrated by British opposition. Mr Major, though a less strident critic of social engineering than Mrs Thatcher, nonetheless remained a considerable irritant. While proceeding with its social charter agenda, the Commission therefore sought an alternative.

Two-Track Social Europe

This brings us to the 'Agreement on Social Policy'. During the 1991 intergovernmental negotiations leading up to the revision of the treaties establishing the common market, the Commission actively sought to extend the reach of social policy, and to widen the treaty basis permitting qualified majority voting beyond the tenuous hold of Article 118A.[10] To this end, it proposed a special social 'chapter' to the proposed new treaty – the Treaty on European Union (or Maastricht Treaty as it is widely known).

British opposition meant that a political compromise was necessary to save the wider treaty. The formula chosen was to relegate the terms of what was to have been the social chapter to a 'Protocol on Social Policy', appended to the Treaty on

---

[9] Thus, changes were introduced into the collective lay-offs directive that made it easier to reach the employment threshold triggering the mandate; the pregnant workers directive was modified to deny member states the right to set eligibility requirements that exceeded one year's length of service; and the working hours directive had initially contained no reference to its most controversial element, the 48-hour week.

[10] Strictly speaking, other treaty bases permitting majority voting at this time were Articles 57(2) and 66, pertaining to self employment and the provision of services; Article 54(3) on right of establishment; and Article 100A on implementing the single market, even if largely undercut by Article 100A(2).

European Union of 1991. Annexed to that Protocol was an Agreement on Social Policy. The Protocol was signed by all 12 member states and noted the intention of 11 of their number to use the machinery of the Community to implement an Agreement on Social Policy; in other words, to pursue a new route to social policy that specifically excluded the UK.

The Agreement marks a watershed in the history of Community labour market regulation. As we shall see, it steps decisively towards a corporatist 'solution' by formally integrating the two sides of industry at European level (the 'social partners') into Community decision-making. It also confirms and clarifies the legal competence of the Community in matters of social policy while extending the basis of majority voting.

As noted earlier, the ambiguity attaching to social policy in the treaties establishing the common market had meant that the Commission was forced to be creative in fixing the authority for its actions. This usually meant justifying its draft legislation in terms of health and safety to avoid the unanimity problem. Although this strategy provided no guarantee of acceptance, it was safer than proceeding under other treaty bases that required unanimity *ab initio*. Now at last the Commission was to have a basis for social policy that could not be legally undercut.

The Agreement on Social Policy sets down five areas where qualified majority voting would apply – as well as another five areas where unanimity was required. Qualified majority voting under the Agreement was permitted for measures covering improvements in the working environment to protect workers' health and safety, working conditions, the information and consultation rights of workers, gender equality, and the integration of persons excluded from the labour market. Hitherto, with the exception of health and safety and gender equality, passage of such measures typically required unanimity. Unanimity would still be required for measures pertaining to social security, dismissals protection, collective representation and codetermination, conditions of employment for third-country nationals resident in the Community, and financial contributions for the promotion of manpower instruments. Of course, with the exclusion of the UK, such unanimity would now be easier to attain.

21

The Agreement on Social Policy does identify some topics that lie outside its competence (legislation on pay, the right to strike/lockout, and the right of association). Draft legislation on such matters would therefore need to be processed by the Commission under the 'social charter route', that is, before all 12 (now 15) member states. But enough has been said to indicate that there were now to be two sets of rules governing social policy in the new European Union.

As we see it, the most revealing aspect of the Agreement on Social Policy is its pronounced corporatist stance: the new role of the social partners in policy formation. This development marked the culmination of a process of 'social dialogue' initiated in 1985 by Jacques Delors. His intention was that such consultations between the two sides of industry would result in agreements that would substitute for Commission mandates.[11]

Even if little practical had emerged from the social dialogue process during the first five years of its life, there was a dramatic change in 1991. In particular, confronted by a mass of actual and proposed social charter legislation and the prospect of a major extension in Community competence as a result of the 1991 deliberations of the inter-governmental conference reviewing the Community constitution – and with it the threat of more intrusive mandates – the employer side abruptly changed tack. After all, might not agreements reached under a process of social dialogue prove less coercive than mandates? An alternative interpretation is that the Maastricht treaty enabled the European Union to grant the social partners a 'deliberate representational monopoly' (Schmitter, 1977, p. 9). On this view, it was not in the interests of the social partners to engage in serious negotiations prior to being granted this *largesse*. In October 1991, the social partners – comprising UNICE and CEEP on the employer side[12] and

---

[11] Note that Article 118B of the SEA subsequently committed the Commission to develop the dialogue between the two sides of industry at European level so that 'relations based on agreement' might emerge if the parties so wished. This was to be long delayed, the two sides of industry issuing a variety of (anodyne) joint opinions rather than entering into collective agreements proper.

[12] UNICE is the French acronym for the private sector Union of Industrial and Employers Confederations of Europe, and CEEP that of the public sector European Centre of Public Enterprises. Together with the ETUC they are but three of the 28 organisations formally consulted by the Commission on legislative proposals covering social policy. Yet they are the 'authorised' social partners.

the European Trade Union Confederation (ETUC) on the labour side – reached agreement on a new form of social dialogue that very closely corresponded with M. Delors's 1985 blueprint.

The terms of the agreement were submitted to the intergovernmental conference and were incorporated to all intents and purposes *verbatim* into the Agreement on Social Policy. The long-standing consultation rights of the social partners were formalised and they were offered the right in effect to take over legislation. The procedure is as follows. *First*, the Commission must consult the partners on the possible direction of Community social and employment policy prior to drawing up any concrete proposal. *Second*, it has again to consult them on the content of any actual proposal. *Third*, at any point in the latter, second-stage consultations the social partners can inform the Commission that they would like to negotiate on the issue. In this case they have nine months to reach an agreement. If agreement is reached, this can be given force of law by a Council directive or decision. *Finally*, if no agreement is reached, the Commission will pursue its own legislative proposals and submit them to the Council in the normal way.

In order to understand the application of the Agreement on Social Policy, a summary of the progress made under the social charter using the more conventional legislative route is required. In the summer of 1994 – immediately prior to the application of the Agreement on Social Policy – of the 26 binding measures stemming from the social charter, some 18 had been enacted into law, another four were either close to passage or seemed assured of eventual passage because of their relatively uncontroversial nature, and just three were deadlocked (including a planned directive on disabled workers that was dormant). Not surprisingly, the three deadlocked measures had a history of controversy: two seeking to regulate part-time work, temporary employment, and fixed-term contracts – rather interestingly termed 'atypical work' by the Commission – and the third to implement transnational works councils in European-scale organisations (see items 10 and 11 of Table 1).

It soon became clear that the Agreement on Social Policy was to be used by the Commission to attend to unfinished business, both in the obvious sense of dealing with blocked social charter measures and also to break the *impasse* on Commission proposals that either long preceded the social charter (in particular, those concerning systems of worker participation) or which were being considered more or less contemporaneously with the social charter but independent of it (for instance, the issue of burden of proof in gender discrimination litigation). In all such cases, the proposals had failed to secure adoption through the formal treaty route. This is not to say that the Commission would necessarily eschew the standard treaty route – in which its proposals would go before the full Council, including the UK – but rather that it would weigh the odds carefully and choose the line of least resistance. Witness the following comment from the (then) Belgian President of the Council of Ministers: 'Although it is preferable to take decisions which are valid in all 12 member states, the procedure of the social protocol will be followed wherever necessary' (see EIRR, 1993, p. 24).

And, as a matter of fact, the Commission was to process a number of social charter and other measures through the formal treaty route. These included the fairly recently adopted measures on posted workers and on equal treatment for men and women in occupational social security schemes,[13] proposed amendments to the 1977 directive on the rights of workers following transfers of ownership of their companies, and the remaining health and safety provisions of the social charter.

The first use of the Agreement on Social Policy was the controversial draft legislation on European Works Councils, initially formally discussed in Council in December 1990 but, as we have seen, in reality dating back to (a component of) the proposal for a European Company Statute some 20 years earlier. This was also the first occasion on which the social partners tried to negotiate their own accord. In the event, they were unable to reach agreement, the union side apparently concluding that a directive would be more favourable to their

---

[13] See, respectively, Council Directive 97/71/EC of the European Parliament and of the Council on the posting of workers in the framework of the provision of services, OC L18 of 21.1.97; Council Directive 96/97/EC of 20 December 1997 amending Directive 86/378/EEC of 24 July 1986 on the implementation of the principle of equal treatment for men and women in occupational social security schemes, OJ L46 of 17.2.97.

members' rights than a collectively-bargained arrangement. The Commission duly presented its own proposals which were adopted by the (reduced) Council in September 1995. (The terms of the legislation are described in item 1 of Table 2.)

But the social partners were able to reach their own framework agreements on parental leave in December 1995, and on part-time work in May 1997. As was noted above, the Commission had first formulated a parental leave mandate in 1983 and its separate proposals on atypical work in 1982 and 1983. The terms of the two framework agreements, reached under Article 3(4) of the Agreement on Social Policy are again detailed in Table 2 (items 2 and 3). Also given in the table are the basic terms of the burden of proof directive, which became law in December 1997 (item 4).

In short, prior to the UK's opt-in there were four pieces of EU legislation actually or virtually in place that did not apply to the UK. But, as we now know, within a month of the 1 May election of a (New) Labour government, the UK signed up to the Agreement on Social Policy which is now part and parcel of the new draft Treaty of Amsterdam, a true social chapter after all.

The Social Chapter Proper

The new Treaty of Amsterdam (drafted in June and signed on 2 October 1997) incorporates the provisions of the Agreement on Social Policy directly into the main body of the Treaty. The Protocol containing that Agreement is thus repealed and the terms of the latter are added to Articles 117 to 120 of the Treaty of Rome. The new Treaty also includes some modest revision of the pre-existing articles dealing with gender, while also containing a new anti-discrimination clause that outlaws discrimination based on gender, race, sexual orientation, age, or disability. More importantly, a major innovation was the introduction of an 'employment chapter' (under Title VIa) into the treaty, details of which are provided in the Box (below, pp. 28-29). Since this initiative opens up scope for considerable Commission activism in the future, we will perforce return to it in what follows.

At the time of signing, it was uncertain just how soon the UK would be on board with respect to legislation processed under the Agreement on Social Policy, because the Amsterdam Treaty would not be ratified until late 1998. But the Commission moved quickly to take up the challenge.
[cont'd on page 29]

Table 2: Measures Processed Under the Agreement on Social Policy

Measure	Content	Status
1. Establishment of European Works Councils (OJ L254 of 30.9.94; OJ L10 of 16.1.98).	Transnational European Works Councils (EWCs) to be set up in undertakings with at least 1,000 employees including at least 150 employees in each of at least two member states. A 'special negotiating body' (SNB) of elected worker representatives to negotiate powers of the EWC with central management. To trigger negotiations requires the written request of at least 100 workers or their representative in at least two undertakings in at least two member states, unless central management initiates negotiations. The SNB can decide, on a two-thirds majority, not to open negotiations or to end them. If negotiations successfully concluded, there are no minimum requirements per se, although the agreement has to cover the scope, composition, membership, and power of the EWC. Where no agreement between SNB and central management 'subsidiary requirements' apply. These cover the size of the EWC, the content of information and consultation, and the number of meetings.	Following breakdown of negotiations between the social partners, the Commission first submitted its proposal to Council in April 1995. Final adoption in Council in September 1995 with implementation by 22 September 1996. Extended to UK on 15 December 1997, with implementation within two years.
2. European Framework Agreement on Parental Leave (OJ L145 of 19.6.96; OJ L10 of 16.1.98).	Parental leave set at three months to be taken until a given age of at least three months to take care of children up to eight years of age, the parameters to be set by the member states or by the social partners. It is not to be transferable between spouses. Job rights to be maintained intact during leave interval. Any qualifying interval for parental leave not to exceed one year of service. No specific reference to income entitlement during leave, which is to be decided at national level.	In July 1995, the social partners informed the Commission that they would begin negotiations. Draft agreement concluded by the social partners in November and formally signed on 14 December 1995. Enforced by a Council Directive on 3 June 1996, with implementation two years thereafter. Extended to the UK on 15 December 1997.

Table 2: Measures Processed Under the Agreement on Social Policy (cont'd.)

Measure	Description	Status
3. European Framework Agreement on Part-time Work (OJ L14 of 20.1.98; OJ L131 of 5.5.98).	Part-time workers (strictly, permanent part-timers) not to be treated in a less favourable manner than their full-time counterparts. Member states can make access to particular conditions of employment subject to a service qualification and to hours/earnings thresholds. Some encouragement given to workers to switch from full-time to part-time work.	Formal talks began in October 1996. Draft agreement concluded in May and formally signed on 6 June 1997. Enforced by a Council Directive on 15 December 1997, and extended to the UK in April 1998, with implementation by April 2001.
4. Burden of Proof in Cases of Discrimination Based on Sex (OJ L14 of 20.1.98).	Directive seeks to 'share' the burden of proof in sex discrimination cases. That is, once the plaintiff shows a series of facts which would, if not rebutted, amount to direct or indirect discrimination, the burden of proof switches to the defendant. (Indirect discrimination is said to exist where a practice simply has a disproportionate effect on a particular group; motive is irrelevant.)	Social partners unable to reach agreement. Processed by Commission. Political agreement reached in Council in June 1997. Formal adoption by Council on 15 December 1997, with implementation scheduled for 1 January 2001. Extended to the UK in July 1998, with implementation by 13 July 2001.
5. National-level Worker Information and Consultation (EIRR, 1998b); OJC2 of 5.1.99.	Harmonization of national schemes for informing and consulting workers.	First-stage consultations began on 4 June 1997; second stage initiated on 5 November 1997, and discussion process extended. Failure of process announced on 16 March 1998. Commission published its proposals in January 1999.
6. Action on Sexual Harassment at Work (EIRR, 1997).	Follow-up to 1991 Commission Resolution on the protection and dignity of women and men at work, and its non-binding recommendation and code of practice on sexual harassment.	First stage consultations with social partners began on 24 July 1996; second stage on 20 March 1997. Social partners unable to reach agreement.

The Employment Chapter of the Amsterdam Treaty

Article B of the Amsterdam treaty identifies 'a high level of employment' as a central objective of the Community. Title VI contains the employment chapter. It commits the Community to developing a co-ordinated strategy for employment, with particular reference to the promotion of a skilled and adaptable labour force and labour markets that are responsive to economic change. It charges the Community with contributing to this high level of employment by supporting and, if necessary, complementing the actions of member states. Moreover, this high employment objective is to be taken into account throughout in the formulation and implementation of Community policies. Specific procedures are established. The European Council of heads of state is to review the employment situation annually, and reach conclusions on the basis of a joint annual report prepared by the Council of Ministers and the Commission (see, for example, Commission, 1997a). Acting on a qualified majority on a proposal from the Commission, the Council is to formulate guidelines that are to be taken into account by the member states in drawing up their employment policies. Member states have to furnish the Council with annual reports on the implementation of their national employment policies in the light of the Council's guidelines. And the Council can in turn make (non-binding) Recommendations to the member states on their performance, again by qualified majority on a recommendation from the Commission. Such Recommendations are duly factored into the joint annual report, submitted to the European Council, on the employment situation and the implementation of the employment guidelines.

Other than this monitoring function, the Council may also adopt 'incentive measures'. These are geared to facilitating co-operation between member states, and take the form of encouraging information exchange, comparative analyses, and pilot projects, and so on. These measures do not yet include harmonisation of national laws and regulations.

In framing its proposals for guidelines, the Commission had initially sought to fix targets for employment and unemployment. Specifically, the aggregate employment rate was to be raised from 60 per cent to 65 per cent within five years, and the unemployment rate to be reduced from 10.6 per cent to 7 per cent over the same interval (Commission, 1997b). These targets were not pursued at the November 1997 summit meeting, but the Council subsequently endorsed four Commission 'guidelines' for member states' employment policies. (Meanwhile, the Community had sanctioned a 'European employment initiative' designed to help small and medium-sized enterprises (SMEs) create jobs and supported a similar, though wider-ranging action plan funded by the European Investment Bank.) The Commission guidelines that were adopted in Council refer to the promotion of a culture of entrepreneurship, that is, more self-employment and new business start-ups; the creation of a culture of employability, seeking, *inter alia*, to ensure that every unemployed adult (young worker) is offered a job, training, retraining, work experience, or other employment-assistance within the first 12 months (6 months) of becoming unemployed; the promotion of adaptability, that is, accommodating to flexible work arrangements with no loss of employment security; and the strengthening of equal opportunities by raising female participation rates via career breaks, parental leave, and the like. Padraig Flynn, DG-V's Commissioner, has categorised these guidelines as tackling 'the jobs gap, the skills gap, the participation gap, and the gender gap' (EIRR, 1998a, p. 20).

Thus, in September 1997, it issued a proposal extending both the European Works Council (EWC) directive and the social partners' framework agreement on parental leave to the UK. Both draft directives were adopted in Council on 15 December without debate. (Note that the mechanism is to re-adopt Agreement on Social Policy legislation on a whole-Community basis under Article 100.) The Commission further noted its intention to offer extension directives for the other two measures processed under the Agreement on Social Policy covering part-time work and the burden of proof (see items 3 and 4 of Table 2). The two measures were duly extended to the UK in 1998 with implementation by 2001.

That still leaves a number of proposals being processed through the Agreement on Social Policy. Their impact on the UK is necessarily unclear until treaty ratification. We refer in particular to Community action on worker information and consultation and sexual harassment at work. The situation has become further clouded with the decision of the private sector employers' confederation, UNICE, to withdraw from negotiations on both sexual harassment at work and the subject of worker involvement and consultation at national level (see items 5 and 6 of Table 2). The Commission is to host a summit meeting of the social partners to address this seeming hiatus in the social dialogue.[14]

---

[14] That being said, the social partners are continuing to hold discussions on the regulation of fixed-term contracts, in a process begun on 23 March 1998.

It is useful to pursue the participation issue in more detail. The issue is involved because there are already a number of pieces of legislation in place covering information and consultation. These comprise the collective redundancies directive (1975, updated in 1992), the directive on transfers of businesses (1977), the 1995 European Works Councils directive, and of course the provisions for worker participation implicit in the large number of Community health and safety laws.

Nevertheless, as we have seen, the Commission has thus far enjoyed little success with what it would regard as its major participation proposals, namely, the Vredeling initiative, the European Company Statute (ECS) and the Fifth Directive on company law. It will be recalled that deliberations on the ECS and the Fifth Directive on company law proceeded alongside the social charter initiatives but were not part of that legislative agenda. They foundered partly because of strong British opposition (the voluntaristic tradition) and material diversity among members states in their procedures for informing and consulting workers.

In its policy statement which formally guides Community policy until 1999, the Commission kept its powder dry on the controversial issue of worker involvement, not identifying any clear line of policy while characteristically seeming unwilling to withdraw any of its past participation initiatives. The subsequently issued medium-term action plan (covering 1995-97) was a little more explicit and it seemed that Vredeling would be withdrawn in the wake of the EWC directive (see, respectively, Commission, 1994, 1995a). A subsequent Commission communication on worker information and consultation, issued in 1995, also implied that the Commission favoured a single new instrument on ways of consulting workers at national level to complement the transnational provisions of the EWC directive (Commission, 1995b).

In June 1997, the Commission launched consultations with the social partners on the subject of possible Community action on worker involvement and consultation (Commission, 1997c). The timing, as is usual with controversial Commission initiatives, is no accident. It followed on (a) the Vilvoorde incident, (b) publication of the Davignon report into worker participation, sponsored by the Commission, and (c) the election in Britain of New Labour. The former incident involved the closure by Renault of its Belgian assembly line in Vilvoorde, allegedly in breach of information and consultation requirements of the EWC directive but more likely offending against national legislation.

For its part, the Davignon report, presented to the Commission in May 1997, focuses solely on the ECS. It recommends that companies setting up as a European Company – an optional form of transnational plc incorporated at European level – voluntarily negotiate a form of participation with their unions. A default penalty in the form of standardised procedures (or 'reference provisions') would otherwise apply. Interestingly, Davignon here retains the worker director component of the old ECS model, although it recommends that workers' representatives have one-fifth (rather than one-third) of the seats on the relevant board (Davignon, 1997).

The Davignon report was incorporated in a revised ECS text that was discussed in the (full) Council in October and again in December 1997. At the time it seemed unlikely that the measure would advance because of the reference provisions on worker directors. But undoubtedly some progress has recently been made in Council by virtue of further amendments to the proposal and, in particular, the insertion of a zero participation option and the removal of a guarantee of board-level representation. This has led some observers to suggest that a (diluted) ECS directive is now close to adoption (EIRR, 1998d).

We have seen that the Commission had begun to progress its proposals seeking to harmonise national-level information and consultation systems under the Agreement on Social Policy. (The ECS is of limited help here because setting up a European Company is not mandatory.) It seeks harmonisation because of the alleged weaknesses of national (and by implication transnational) mechanisms of informing and consulting workers, the need to avoid 'distortions of competition' while supposedly increasing the competitiveness of firms, as well as the need to render existing arrangements more transparent and consistent (Commission, 1997d). It was on this unusually imprecise basis that the Commission began consultations with the social partners in June 1997. We earlier noted UNICE's withdrawal from what had been an extended consultation process in March 1998. At the time of writing, the Commission has just published its own proposals for a framework of minimum Community standards for informing and consulting employees (OJC2 of 5.1.99).

Other Social Policy Developments

Apart from processing a number of relatively uncontroversial measures, such as proposals seeking to safeguard the pension rights of workers moving within the Community and a health and safety directive covering exposure to physical agents,[15] the main initiatives being pursued by the Commission at the beginning of 1998 were an extension of the social charter working time directive, the regulation of atypical work, employment protection in the context of individual (as opposed to collective) dismissals, and, of course, action on national systems of worker involvement and consultation. The first measure seeks to extend the terms of the 1993 working time directive (item 9, Table 1) to areas excluded from the scope of that instrument, namely, air, rail, and sea transportation, offshore activities, and trainee doctors. The Commission calculates that these excluded sectors and activities account for around 5.6 million jobs, or 4 per cent of total employment in the EU. It will offer a mix of general rules for extension and specific legislation targeted at individual sectors (Commission, 1997e). By analogy with the abortive discussions on sexual harassment, the Commission will offer its own draft proposals on atypical work if the social partners' consultations on fixed-term contracts, initiated in March 1998, fail to lead to agreement.

Action on individual dismissals has been signalled by Padraig Flynn (EIRR, 1998a, p. 22). Any such initiative has to be seen in the light of the recent appointment of an external group of experts, charged with examining the economic and

---

[15] See, respectively, OJC5 of 9.1.98 and OJC230 of 13.9.93. The Commission will presumably also move to secure adoption of its proposals updating the 1977 transfer of undertakings directive establishing worker rights in the event of transfers of businesses (see Proposal for a Council Directive on the approximation of the laws of the member states relating to the safeguarding of employees' rights in the event of transfers of undertakings, businesses or parts of businesses, OJ C274 of 1.10.94). Its current proposals reflect the large body of case law emanating from the European Court of Justice since 1977.

social implications of industrial change – a procedure followed earlier by the Commission preparatory to its proposals on worker participation (and occupational pensions). Its remit is to analyse likely industrial changes and to consider ways of better anticipating them so as to guard against their economic and social effects (Gyllenhammar, 1998).

The vagueness of the policy document setting out the main lines of EU social policy up to 1999, its recognition that a 'solid base' of Community social legislation was already in place, and its seeming emphasis on jobs rather than social rights (Commission, 1994) might after all suggest that DG-V has lost its reformist zeal. But the contrast with the detail of the social charter (and its accompanying Action Programme) is more apparent than real. True, there has been something of a lull in legislative activity in recent years, but it was logical for the directorate not to commit to a raft of new legislation at a time when Europe was preoccupied with its reduced competitiveness and the continuing upward drift in unemployment (see Commission, 1993). In other words, the economic constraints facing DG-V in 1994 were very nearly binding. What more sensible at this time than to offer a policy that focused on consolidation, implementation, consultation, and even analysis. Or to devise a 'rolling' action programme (Commission, 1995a), short on detail but with the ability to take advantage of the circumstances of time and place – Vilvoorde providing a classic example – to push forward specific policies.

But now circumstances are clearly running in the Commission's favour. With ratification of the Treaty of Amsterdam, the Agreement on Social Policy will formally become a social chapter, providing an unambiguous treaty basis for social policy on equal footing with the goal of economic union. Any lessening of the economic constraints on the Commission will occasion vigorous application of EU-wide mandates. The necessary array of constituencies is in place. The conduct of social policy will be messier in the future, partly by reason of the necessarily partial and piecemeal actions of the social partners in pursuing policies desired by the Commission, but this is a potential source of strength rather than weakness for an activist Commission. The corporatist solution is the foot in the door when progress on the most controversial measures is required. It also smacks of

33

consensus and flexibility but the end-goal has still to be seen as one of unalloyed labour market re-regulation.

At the time of writing, the Commission has just published its Social Action Programme for 1998-2000 (Commission, 1998). Like its post-social charter precursors, the document is again somewhat thin on detail. But it is clear that the Commission sees the employment chapter as very much a central plank of social policy, providing among other things the basis for major new education and training programmes (on which, see Addison and Siebert, 1994), and not simply incentive measures. A second broad theme of the programme is the organisation of work (see Commission, 1997f). Here the Commission emphasises the need to promote flexibility, albeit with no loss in worker security. Concrete measures include a formal extension of the working time directive (noted earlier), legislation on the protection of teleworkers, consolidation and adaptation of existing health and safety directives, and the erection of minimum standards for national information and consultation. The latter initiative is couched in terms of the need to anticipate industrial change, which rubric also heralds new legislation on EWCs. Abstracting from issues of social exclusion, a final theme of the action programme is the external dimension of policy. In part this covers 'assistance' to new entrants to the European Union in the full implementation of existing and future social policy legislation. Not surprisingly, this external dimension also embraces the active promotion of core labour standards in international trade by involving both the International Labour Organisation and the World Trade Organisation.

III. Rationale

The mandating of minimum labour standards raises similar issues to the introduction of minimum wages. In both cases the cost of labour is increased, so there is the problem that employment might fall. Yet also in both cases market failure arguments can be made to support intervention. The basic question is: Under what circumstances can government mandates improve on freedom of contract between individuals? Let us first consider how free markets work to establish wages and working conditions, before addressing various forms of market failure.

The Competitive Process

According to conventional economic theory, workers seek jobs offering the mix of wages and working conditions which suit them best. Working conditions which are generally liked, such as employment security, then tend to be associated with lower wages. Conversely, jobs with unfavourable conditions (for example, risk of death down a mine) tend to have higher wages. A 'wage locus' such as that shown in Figure 1 emerges.

The wage locus in Figure 1 illustrates the idea that a worker commands a particular 'full wage', given his/her education. There are different full wages, and different loci for each level of education, as shown. The full wage is defined as the sum of the money wage plus the worker's valuation of the job's working conditions. Competition among firms for workers, combined with worker preferences, is meant to ensure that jobs with bad conditions offer a positive compensating wage differential (CWD).[16] The converse applies for jobs with good conditions. The 'law of one price' in the labour market

---

[16] Both the distribution of worker preferences (the supply side) and the number of jobs with bad conditions (the demand side) will determine the size of the CWD. For example, if there are few jobs with high workplace accident risk, then it will be possible to fill these jobs with workers who – perhaps because they are used to such jobs – are not averse to the risk. In such cases the CWD will be low to non-existent. Conversely, where many firms require workers to fill dangerous jobs, the CWD will be high.

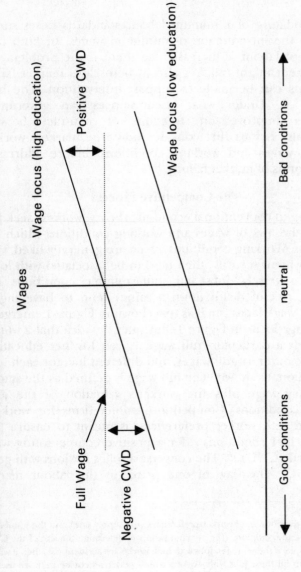

Figure 1: The Wages and Working Conditions Trade-off

requires that the full wage is the same across different jobs for workers of given education. The wage locus thus gives the opportunity set for workers of given education.

Workers will choose a position on the wage locus according to their tastes and their wealth. Wealth will be important because the rich can more easily afford to be 'choosy'. By contrast, unskilled workers – who can command only a low full wage – will need to take jobs with poorer conditions because the positive CWD will make it easier for them to make ends meet. Lack of resources tends to force poorer workers (and indeed poorer countries) to choose jobs with less favourable working conditions. Because the workers are doing the best that they can, assuming perfect competition and information, there is nothing to be particularly concerned about here. Nevertheless, it does follow that mandating improved working conditions will require most adjustment on the part of the unskilled workers – who have selected the poor conditions – not their skilled counterparts. It is primarily the unskilled workers' opportunity set which is restricted; the right-hand section of the wage locus in Figure 1 is made illegal.

In a competitive world, working conditions are meant to be determined by a process of *tâtonnement* ('groping') so that a position is reached which makes both sides as well off as possible. The process is illustrated in Figure 2, taking workplace safety as an example (see also Addison and Siebert, 1993). Suppose that the *tâtonnement* process has resulted in a risk of injury r=r*. Accordingly, demand is illustrated in the diagram as D|r=r* and supply as S|r=r*. Equilibrium is at B, and the wage is W_1. Point B should maximise the sum of profits (triangle ABW_1) and worker surplus (triangle W_1BF); it will then also maximise employment.

In such circumstances, can mandating more safety improve on outcome B? One possibility is shown in Figure 2. Mandating greater safety expenditures will shift the net demand curve (that is, after taking account of safety expenditures) down to D|mandate. The extra safety expenditures act like a tax. The supply curve will also shift downwards because workers presumably prefer working in safer firms, and therefore will accept lower wages. Let us suppose that the supply curve shifts more than does the demand curve, resulting in a move to a position like C which is preferable to B. Employment is higher and the sum of worker

37

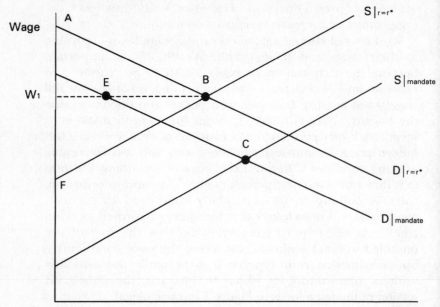

Figure 2: Wage and Employment Effects of Mandates

surplus and firm profit is higher. C is a Pareto improvement on B: everyone is better off at C than at B. The diagram could also be drawn to illustrate the case where the workers do not value the mandate as much as it costs firms. In this case, employment will fall. Note that, in any event, the money wage must fall when the mandate is imposed. If wages do not fall, a move to a position such as E is implied, offering lower employment than B.

Figure 2 suggests that if the costs of a safety mandate are less than the benefits, as evaluated by workers, then employment will rise. Accordingly, the employment effect of the mandate provides a simple test of whether benefits outweigh costs.

A problem with this simple employment test, however, is that it does not allow for distributional issues. Figure 2 assumes that labour is homogeneous. But it is possible to imagine situations where employment declines, but sufficient benefits nonetheless accrue to 'deserving' individuals to offset the damage done to others. In particular, if unskilled, poor workers gain employment at the expense of the better off, a safety law reducing overall employment would be more

38

acceptable than otherwise. The employment test therefore needs to be supplemented by consideration of who becomes unemployed. Such distributional effects will be controversial, particularly if they work to offset employment effects. The question is whether deserving recipients of 'fundamental social rights', that is, the poor and unskilled, can take advantage of them.

In practice, it is likely that unskilled workers will be disadvantaged by mandates, for three reasons. *First*, it is necessary for the wage to fall when a mandate is imposed; otherwise, as we have seen, employment will decline. However, it is typically the case that unskilled wages are too close to minimum wage or unemployment benefit floors to be able to fall much – increasing the unemployment risk for the unskilled. *Second*, unskilled workers are more likely to be employed in small firms.[17] It is small firms which have the worst working conditions (for example, accident rates are much higher in small firms), and which will therefore be most affected by mandates. Hence, the firms employing the unskilled will have to make the biggest adjustments – again increasing the unemployment risk for the unskilled. *Third*, the unskilled are more likely to 'take advantage' of mandates: for example, to take time off sick. This will make the personnel office more wary of hiring the unskilled, and thereby reduce their employment opportunities.

In sum, it seems that many mandates will tend to sharpen the distinction between skilled 'insiders' and the more vulnerable 'outsider' groups of the young, the inexperienced, and the uneducated. If the unskilled are likely to be disadvantaged by a mandate, then the issue of whether there are equity gains to offset efficiency (or employment) losses does not arise. We can use the simple employment test in Figure 2 after all.

Figure 2 illustrates the conditions that must be met if a mandate is to increase employment and make both sides

---

[17] The General Household Survey, a national survey of about 10,000 households, shows that 71 per cent of uneducated young men under 25 (without 'O' or 'A' levels, or tertiary education) work in small plants (under 100 workers). The figure for educated young men is lower, 56 per cent, and that for prime-age men lower still, 30–40 per cent, according to education. (Special tabulation from the 1992 GHS data tapes.)

better off. At the same time it raises the question of why, if a position such as C exists which is preferred to B, the parties have not independently discovered it in the first place. Why do they need government help?

Arguments for Intervention

Conventional economic theory recognises that there may be obstacles to workers and firms negotiating surplus-maximising (or employment-maximising) contracts. These obstacles are termed 'market failures'. We will take up three main types of market failure here: monopsony, externalities, and imperfect (and asymmetric) information.

Monopsony: Monopsony means 'single buyer', by analogy with monopoly meaning 'single seller'. To the extent that workers lack mobility, they become subject to the single-buyer or monopsony power possessed by firms. If a firm has such power, it will restrict employment and in a technical sense 'exploit' its workers by offering a wage and working conditions package worth less than their contribution to the firm (their marginal revenue product). In terms of Figure 2, the firm will notionally stay at a point such as B to the left of C – even though employment growth would be Pareto-improving in the sense that expansion would benefit workers more than the firm loses.

In general, the competitive market model depends upon workers' powers of 'exit', that is, on their threat to move between firms to take up better offers. Therefore, the issue of the obstructions to worker choice which confer monopsony power on firms is fundamental.

Monopsony need not be restricted to the 'company town' of the textbooks. There are many reasons – including specific human capital investments in a firm, or family ties – why workers cannot be instantaneously mobile. In the short run, all firms have monopsony power. (The issue of workers' monopoly power, stemming from their private knowledge about the work process, is taken up below.) But the more relevant question concerns the responsiveness of workers to wage differentials over the medium to long term. Econometric estimates for US hospitals indicate that the one-year elasticity of labour supply to a hospital is low (Boal and Ransom, 1997, p. 105). It is around 1.3 – a 10 per cent increase in the wage only brings about a 13 per cent increase in employment.

40

However, the three-year elasticity is 4.0 (a 10 per cent increase in the wage now bringing about a 40 per cent increase in employment over three years), and the long-run elasticity is approximately infinite. A UK study of elasticity of labour supply to residential care homes for the elderly reported a long-run elasticity of about 25.0 (Machin *et al.*, 1993).

Results from monopsony studies are summarised in Table 3. The extent to which wages deviate from marginal revenue product (MRP) is shown, as well as the long-run labour supply elasticity where available. The first two rows give results for US baseball players and football players. These sports examples are classic monopsony markets where rules prevent players from moving among clubs. Even here, the rate of 'exploitation' (as measured by the ratio of the MRP to the wage) seems to be low, ranging from zero to 20 per cent. Exploitation in the case of university staff is also interesting because this is another group which might face barriers to mobility (due to specific investments in particular universities). Exploitation for this group is estimated by measuring the wage premium that recently-moved staff earn over non-moving staff with the same qualifications and publication record. The rate of exploitation is again quite low, ranging from 5 per cent to 18 per cent. Finally, the studies of US hospitals and UK residential care homes are summarised. The values given in the table support the competitive model, as already noted. Boal and Ransom (1997, p. 110) themselves conclude that monopsony exploitation is 'probably widespread but small on average'.

A fundamental difficulty with resting the case for mandates on the firm monopsony-power argument is that monopsony rarely occurs alone. Workers also have (varying) degrees of monopoly power since all jobs are to some extent unique or 'idiosyncratic'. The importance of worker power is shown by the pervasiveness of internal labour market practices such as promotion from within. Such internal labour markets 'tie the interests of the worker to the firm in a continuing way' (Williamson *et al.*, 1975, p. 273) because the worker can only advance via internal promotion. Internal labour markets are needed to suppress worker opportunism, and to ensure that workers do not 'hoard information to their personal advantage and engage in a series of bilateral monopolistic exchanges with the management' (Williamson *et al.*, 1975, p. 257).

Table 3: Findings on Monopsony

Group	Ratio of marginal revenue product to wage	Long-run elasticity of labour supply
Baseball players	1.20	
American football players	1.0	
US college professors	1.05 to 1.18	
US hospitals over six years	1.04 to 1.13	Approx. infinite; three-year elasticity is 4.0
UK residential homes for elderly	1.15	25

Notes: Marginal revenue product (MRP) measures labour productivity and equals the wage if firms are in competitive labour markets (elasticity of supply is infinite).
Source: Boal and Ransom (1997).

While formal econometric studies of worker power (aside from union power) are clearly difficult to undertake, the fact that long-term contracts are the norm for workers in the UK is significant. The average UK male worker's job lasts about 20 years, and for females the figure is 12 years. Despite popular impressions to the contrary, these long job tenures have not declined over time (Burgess and Rees, 1996). For many if not most workers, therefore, we can take it that freedom of contract is not materially dented by potential monopsony power.

Externalities: Externalities are non-priced (or poorly-priced) goods, pollution being the clearest example. Externalities are caused by missing or poorly functioning markets; for example, the market for air. In the labour market, there are many possibilities, including training (firms poaching trained workers), public goods aspects of working conditions, advance notice (benefits to communities in which closing plants are located), parental leave (healthier children and hence more productive adults), and second-best arguments for notice and severance pay based on imperfect unemployment insurance (UI) rating. (UI payments are not higher for firms with above-average redundancies, thereby encouraging unstable employment.)

Arguments based on externalities in the labour market are controversial. Whether markets are poorly functioning or not tends to be a matter of judgement. In the case of workplace safety, for example, it can be argued that a worker's learning about the safety implications of a particular industrial process will be beneficial to the workforce as a whole – it is a public good. Because the workforce will not pay the worker for acquiring this knowledge an externality arises: workers learn less about safety than they should, because they are inadequately compensated for so doing (Krueger, 1994, p. 302). On the other hand, it can be argued that workers effectively penalise unsafe workplaces by requiring higher pay (the wage locus of Figure 1). Firms therefore have an incentive to learn about the safety aspects of their industrial processes. Given that the wage locus appears to have a steep slope (see Siebert and Wei, 1994), the incentive for the employer to be informed appears to be strong, effectively disposing of this externality case. But some labour market 'externalities' are even more controversial than this. Training is a case in point.

Externalities are often said to arise in the case of training. Firms make training investments hoping to recoup these investments later by paying trained workers less than their value on the open market. In these circumstances, trained workers are likely to be 'poached' by other firms, because the value of the training is not fully reflected in the worker's wage. A prisoner's dilemma is said to emerge. Firms, realising the possibility of poaching, refuse to train (or under-train) their workforces even though a preferred 'high training–high productivity' equilibrium would be attainable in the absence of poaching. An appropriate solution here might be to neutralise the poaching threat, either by requiring all firms to train (though how 'training' is then defined and monitored is a leading question), or forcing the non-training firms to subsidise their training counterparts.

One objection to the training externalities argument as formulated above is that it relies on some form of prior wage inflexibility. There has to be some obstacle (for example, a minimum wage law, or high welfare benefits) to trainees accepting wages low enough to reflect their 'share' of training benefits. If trainees could accept low wages, they would in effect be paying for their own training investments, and poaching would no longer be of concern to the firm. Trained workers would then need to be paid more than non-trained. Training would have a market price, and the externality would disappear. Instead of a cumbersome training mandate, the answer might be more wage flexibility in the form of, say, a sub-minimum wage for young workers.

It has been argued that the flexible wages argument ignores not only firm monopsony power but also the uncertainties of calculating the benefits and costs of training for both parties (Stevens, 1996). These difficulties do not arise in the case of completely general training. Given that general training raises productivity in many firms, there is no question of monopsony. In addition, it is clear that the trainee receives all the benefits (productivity is raised everywhere) and so will pay for all the costs. Where the training has a firm-specific element the position is not so simple. Because the training is specific, the worker's choices are limited to a small set of firms. Each member firm within the set then achieves potential monopsony power over the worker and wishes to attract and exploit him/her. Moreover, given that the training is specific, it would not make sense for the worker to pay all the costs since he/she could only gain from the investment in a few firms; the training firm also has to have a stake in the training.

The question is whether a contract can be written which will simultaneously protect the worker from the firm's monopsony power and protect the firm's investment in the worker. According to Becker (1964), the answer is simple: the contract must specify that both sides share in the costs and returns of the training investment. Then the worker's threat to negate the firm's investment by quitting protects the worker's wage. And the worker's promised share in the returns gives the worker an incentive to remain with the firm, thereby protecting the firm's investment. The internal labour market with its long-term contracts appears to provide this type of risk-sharing arrangement.

But there are difficulties with the sharing argument, too. No training is completely specific or completely general, and uncertainties arise, for both sides, as to what the alternative value of the training is. What should the worker's 'share' be? And will the firm's concern with its reputation be sufficient to ensure it pays back the worker's share through higher wages? Markets may be 'thin' for some types of specific training. Conventions as to the terms for sharing need not then be established. For example, suppose that initially only a single firm demands particular skills. When such a firm begins operations it will start training workers, so eventually generating a supply of skilled workers which in turn may benefit other firms. Because of the uncertainties, the trainees might not accept a lower wage in return for future higher wages. Hence the firm will not necessarily be compensated for its training efforts, and an externality arises causing insufficient training. The uncertainties involved in specific training may thus reduce the opportunities for profitable investment.

However, while it is theoretically possible for certain externalities to arise in the case of training, that is not to say that they do arise. As it is, the state already intervenes extensively in the provision of training, spending over 0.5 per cent of GDP in the case of the UK, and more in other EU states (see Table 10, below, p. 70). It has yet to be demonstrated that such subsidies are necessary as a result of market failure – or, indeed, whether the amount of the subsidy corresponds in any way to the extent of the failure. Moreover, such state programmes have many practical difficulties, including deadweight losses (subsidising workers who would have been trained anyway), substitution losses (the subsidised worker displacing the unsubsidised), what to train workers for, and how to monitor schemes which have no easily defined unit of output. Questions of justifying such massive programmes, and making them more effective, go far beyond theoretical niceties regarding training externalities.[18] And, as we have seen, the employment chapter promises all sorts of additional training subventions.

18 *Editor's note.* A discussion of whether government spending on training is justified is in J.R. Shackleton, *Training Too Much?*, Hobart Paper 118, London: Institute of Economic Affairs, 1992.

Worker Misinformation: If workers lack information, then the compensating wage differentials associated with the various types of working conditions illustrated in Figure 1 will tend to disappear. The question of whether there are such compensating wage differentials has generated a large literature (see Siebert and Wei, 1994). Many results, but by no means all, are generally consistent with Figure 1. The exceptions might be related to the fact that working conditions are difficult to measure. Moreover, individuals' tastes can differ regarding 'good' and 'bad' conditions. On balance, there does not seem much hard evidence to support the belief that workers *systematically* make mistakes in assessing working conditions.

Asymmetric Information (Adverse Selection): There is also the issue of firms' ignorance as to the quality of their workers. What is the true health status, or pregnancy risk, or diligence of new recruits? Personnel tests are available to assess these matters, but a margin of error naturally remains because workers know more about their own qualities than does the firm: they have private information unavailable to the firm so that we speak of information being asymmetric. For this reason, firms might be reluctant to offer company health insurance – even though their workers would value such insurance, and the company could provide it more cheaply than the workers could buy it for themselves (see Summers, 1989). The difficulty from the firm's point of view is that if it alone offers insurance it will tend to attract the bad risks. Adverse selection operates. In terms of Figure 2, fear of adverse selection prevents point C being attained. However, if all firms are forced to offer insurance under a mandate, adverse selection evaporates because risks can be pooled.

The adverse selection argument can be used as a basis for wide-ranging insurance-type mandates. Not only company health insurance, and maternity protection, but also procedures providing protection against 'unfair' dismissal can be embraced by the argument. Unfair dismissal procedures mean 'due process' in dismissal, and would include provision for third-party arbitration in the event of a dispute over dismissals, and/or delegation of co-determination power over dismissal issues to a works council. Such co-determination procedures provide a form of insurance for workers in bad times. The procedures would also reassure workers, and stimulate their disclosure of private information on aspects of the workplace. Nevertheless, firms may be deterred from setting up such valuable procedures because of fears of adverse selection (that is, being swamped by the less diligent type of worker). Mandates enforcing worker participation and works councils can thus be given a market failure basis.

There are two main difficulties with the adverse selection argument. *First*, it is difficult to establish empirical support for it. In the case of dismissal protection, for example, it is true that workplaces with such protection ('participative' workplaces) appear to exhibit higher labour productivity (Ichnowski *et al.*, 1997; Addison *et al.*, 1997). However, all this shows is that these particular firms are optimising. Without experimental data, we cannot definitely conclude that firms without participative procedures would do better if they had them.

Second, mandates reduce variety in contracts. Yet some firms – and, in particular, small firms – are likely to have greater need to screen out at-risk groups such as unhealthy or lazy workers. Imposing a mandate can prevent such firms deterring the high-risk groups by offering a 'no-frills' contract. Variety in contracts is needed to cater for the many different types of firm in an economy (for a formal treatment see Addison *et al.*, 1998). Mandates, if they are to be introduced, will need to have many exceptions and different levels. In sum, it is one thing to identify a potential source of market failure, another to determine its extent and severity, and quite another to devise appropriate remedies (raising the prospect of government failure).

The relevance of the market failure argument is that it may counter the presumption that mandates cost jobs or, more formally, cause welfare losses. Thus, for example, if firms are forced to provide a service that workers value at more than its cost of provision, employment will actually increase in the wake of a mandate because the wage will fall in a greater amount, other things being equal. But, to repeat, wages must be flexible downward. The other side of the coin, however, is that where the mandated benefit is valued at less than its costs of provision, then even flexible wages will not prevent employment from falling (see Figure 2).

Redistribution: Efficiency is not the only criterion for judging mandates. Equity considerations may indeed be accorded greater priority. Society may well prefer to achieve a redistribution in favour of its poorer members. But the issue is whether the poor are advantaged by such moves and whether there are not more efficient redistributive mechanisms (for example, earned income tax credits versus minimum wages). We have already noted that the logic of mandates is that they will adversely affect job opportunities for the unskilled, and sharpen insider-outsider distinctions. The logic of mandates is that they are more likely to be regressive than progressive.

An arresting example of such regressivity is the hours limitation mandate (item 9 of Table 1). The mandate is built on the proposition that workers are forced (because of employers' monopsony power?) to work for longer hours than they wish. Alternatively, workers might be thought to be mis-informed, and work longer than is 'good for them'. Yet in practice the mandate will only be enforced in respect of those who work standard weeks, that is, primarily the hourly-paid workers. Professional and managerial workers will be free to work as many hours of overtime as they wish – and advance their careers and incomes in the process. Thus, it is mainly the lower-paid workers whose hours will be limited. Also, unless the hourly wage rate for the low-paid increases fully to offset their hours reduction, which is unlikely, lower-paid workers' earnings will fall. The higher-paid will be unaffected. We conclude that the hours limitation mandate is regressive.

The Commission might be coming to an acceptance of these issues. Its recent emphasis on an 'employment chapter' (see previous section) suggests that it is trying to mop up the unemployment induced by certain of its mandates. In other words, the realisation is growing that mandates might have hurt those whom they were intended to help.

Destructive Competition: A further argument rests on the notion of 'destructive competition'. In essence, the argument is that it is wrong for countries to compete on the basis of different social standards, which will produce a levelling down of such standards at the expense of workers. Low standards countries produce a negative externality, as it were, for the high standards countries. The process is often termed 'social dumping' and is widely condemned in Europe; for example, when the Hoover plant in Dijon, France, was relocated to Cumbernauld in Scotland on the grounds that non-wage costs were considerably lower in the latter location, the decision was roundly attacked by the French political establishment as social dumping.

Social dumping is a long-discredited argument going back to League of Nations days. Poorer countries have to compete on the basis of lower wages and conditions. Remove this advantage and their principal competitive edge evaporates. It is surely no accident that the poorer nations of the Community only accepted social charter legislation raising their labour costs after they had received the promise of much increased subventions from the Community's structural funds.[19] The major increase in the social funds – the bulk of which went to the lagging regions – after the treaty revisions of 1988 and 1993 are more to be seen as compensation to the poorer member states, for acquiescing in the erosion of their competitive position by reason of actual and future harmonisation costs, than as reflecting the convergence criteria under monetary union.

There is no justification for the argument that harmonisation of social standards is a logical precursor of economic integration. Rather, harmonisation is likely to be the net outcome of a process of economic integration. Social standards are akin to normal goods (the demand for which rises with income). As countries become richer, they are likely to demand higher standards of health and safety in the workplace. (If we nonetheless find ambitious standards in poorer countries to begin with, we would infer that the laws are not enforced; this inference is in fact supported in the data.) It need not be denied that individual member states might themselves feel that factors such as 'social partnership' facilitate growth – although ambitious social systems ultimately have to stand a market test – merely that the process of economic integration does not require harmonisation of national welfare states. Thus, for example, the dramatic upswing of trade between the United States and Europe was not based on *ex ante* harmonisation, any more for that matter

---

[19] By 1992, Portugal, Greece, and Ireland were receiving annually as much as 3.5 per cent, 2.9 per cent, and 2.3 per cent of their respective GDPs from these funds.

than was the main thrust towards integration in the common market as it then was (Paqué, 1997).

The destructive competition argument is indicative of the DG-V's distrust of markets. This is manifested more generally in its attempts to 'second-guess' firms. Statements to the effect that 'Community action should be more future-oriented to anticipate and cushion change', and 'must be concentrated to a greater extent on a few, key, multi-sectoral technologies' (Commission, 1992, pp. 25-6) imply that the Community can somehow anticipate change, and decide on R&D directions better than can business. Some well-meaning pressure groups go further, of course. Statements such as

> 'Effective labour standards constitute a form of discipline for firms, requiring them to engage in continuous improvements to products and techniques in order to stay competitive.' (Ewing, 1996, p. 26)

are unfortunately typical.

The contention that business, left to its own devices, will anticipate change and be cost effective in the field of R&D, *inter alia*, can of course be countered by the argument that market imperfections require intervention. Perhaps the issue is ultimately empirical (see next section). But to us, the idea that government officials – with no real stake in the outcome of their decisions – can be better at forecasting than private firms whose existence depends on correct decision-making belongs in the realm of Alice in Wonderland.

To conclude: in evaluating mandates the following issues have to be addressed. *First*, one has to identify, in the manner of Table 4, the sources of market failure that the policies are designed to correct. Table 4 summarises the possible market failure arguments that could be deployed to defend the main EU directives. The difficulties associated with these arguments have to be squarely confronted. *Second*, one has further to specify the parameters of individual mandates. *Third*, one has to move from theory (and specification) to policy. It cannot be presumed that the government can be relied upon to correct matters. Only if the cost of market failure outweighs the cost of potential government failure is the mandate indicated on efficiency grounds.

The principal source of government failure – apart from self-seeking behaviour on the part of the bureaucracy and

Table 4: Mandates and 'Market Failure'

Directive	*Possible market failure justification*	*Explanation*
Training	Externalities	Firms might 'poach' trained workers.
Health and safety	Mis-information, monopsony, externalities	Workers might be unaware of hazards – partly because safety information is a public good – and also perhaps be forced into dangerous work due to lack of mobility, etc.
Collective redundancies	Mis-information, externalities	Prior notice might enable workers to search better. Might also be second-best benefits.
Written contracts	Mis-information, monopsony	Workers might be unaware of contract terms, and also perhaps be forced to accept unfair terms due to lack of mobility.
Child labour	Mis-information, myopia	Young workers and their parents might be poorly informed about the benefits of education (a type of merit goods argument).
Posted workers	'Destructive' competition (negative externalities across countries)	If posted workers do not receive host country wages and conditions, this bids down wages and conditions.
Pregnant workers	Asymmetric information	Fear of adverse selection might prevent firms setting up maternity leave schemes.
Working hours	Monopsony, mis-information/myopia	Lack of choice might force workers to work over-long hours. Workers might not know what is good for them.
Atypical workers	'Destructive' competition	Some countries encourage atypical work, which might give them an unfair advantage.
European works councils	Asymmetric information	Fear of adverse selection might prevent firms setting up co-determination schemes; there might also be externalities from 'traditional' firms.

politicians – is informational, for reasons associated with the heterogeneity of markets and market participants. This latter consideration assumes even greater importance in a pan-European setting given the diversity of the constituent market economies. Here, the need to examine the specifics of the market failure argument is most clearly underlined: since market failures will differ between countries, this can only undermine the case on welfare grounds for harmonisation.

Efficiency is not the only justification for mandates. There is also the question of equity. ('Social consensus' can also be interpreted in an equity light.) Indeed, equity appears by default to be the principal basis for Commission activity in the area of social policy. Two major issues are posed here. *First*, among those in work, the disadvantaged appear more likely to be harmed than helped by mandates placing floors under working conditions. This prediction follows logically because mandates will disrupt mainly low-wage labour markets. *Second*, measures that may notionally increase earnings equality may not do the same for incomes in the presence of disemployment effects. Here the fundamental question is whether the focus should be upon employment mandates that benefit only those in employment. It is all too easy, therefore, to envisage mandates that are the worst of both worlds, serving to increase both inefficiency and inequality.

IV. Empirical Research Into the Effects of Labour Market Mandates

There is a considerable literature seeking to identify the impact of regulation on employment outcomes. As we demonstrated earlier in connection with Figure 2, positive employment outcomes provide a basic test of the economic efficiency of mandates. The test is certainly not the last word because it assumes that labour is homogeneous. For this reason, it is necessary to pay particular attention to employment opportunities for the least skilled. In what follows, we first take up the issue of how to measure labour market regulation, and then consider the extant empirical evidence.

As an introduction, however, it is worth considering a simple indicator of employment 'success' in the UK, namely, the trend in the employment/population ratio. Generally speaking, the higher this ratio, and the more it has increased over time, the greater are the employment opportunities being generated by the economy. An alternative indicator would be the unemployment rate, but this is more difficult to make comparable over time owing to frequent changes in definition (though rigorous analyses of unemployment are considered below). Two groups are considered in Table 5, namely, prime-age workers aged 25-54 years, and 55-64 year olds. The young worker, 15-24 group, is omitted for measurement reasons, because many such individuals are trainees in government schemes and therefore have an ambiguous employment status. Statistics are presented for the UK, Japan, and the US, together representing less regulated economies, as well as the main EU states each of which is more strictly regulated. (Details of regulation are considered below.)

For males, the picture presented in Table 5 is of a broad decline in employment/population ratios across countries over the last 15 years. The decline is most marked – 8 percentage points – for the older males. In the case of women, by contrast, the average trend in employment/population ratios is upward for the prime-age 25-54 group, though a slight decline is evident for older women. The UK is perceptibly

Table 5: Changes in Employment-Population Ratios by Sex and Age (%)

		Average of 1979 and 1983		Average of 1990 and 1996		Change 1979/83 to 1990/96	
		25-54	55-64	25-54	55-64	25-54	55-64
France	Men	92	58	88	41	-4	-17
	Women	60	34	67	29	7	-5
Germany	Men	91	60	86	50	-5	-10
	Women	53	26	63	23	10	-3
Italy	Men	91	a	87	47	5	a
	Women	37	10	47	14	10	4
Netherlands	Men	86	54	89	43	3	-11
	Women	a	a	57	18	a	a
UK	Men	90	63[b]	88	60	-2	-3
	Women	59	33[b]	70	38	11	5
Japan	Men	95	81	95	80	0	-1
	Women	65	45	63	47	7	2
US	Men	89	68	88	65	-1	-3
	Women	61	39	72	46	11	7
Average change 1979/83 to 1990/96:					Men	-2	-8
					Women	9	-2

Notes: [a] Changes in definition over time make comparisons unreliable.
   [b] Figure is for 1984 (not the average for 1979 and 1983).

Sources: OECD (1994), Table 7.9; OECD (1996), Table B; OECD (1997), Table C.

better than average, with little change in the employment-population ratios of men, and increases for women. UK trends are quite similar to those in the US and Japan. The regulated economies do worse. France, in particular, has had steeper-than-average declines in employment-population ratios and a smaller than average increase for prime age women. Note, too, the marked declines for men in Germany. Although Table 5 in no sense proves that labour regulation is bad for employment, it does show that the case may have some *prima facie* foundation. We can be reasonably confident that the UK, whatever its other failings, has generated more jobs than its major EU competitors.

Measuring Regulation

Studies of labour regulation proceed by devising a measure of the 'strictness' of regulation, and then relating it to employment and other outcomes. For example, a simple approach used in early British studies was to construct a time series of the number of unfair dismissal cases. An alternative method is to survey employers as to their perceptions of the severity of the regulatory climate. Thus, in a series of European Commission-funded surveys, employers have been asked about 'the importance of hiring and firing laws as an obstacle to employing more people' (see Table 7, below, p. 58). Such measures can be criticised as rather unsophisticated, however, and certainly the surveys of employers have shown some inconsistency over time.

A more satisfactory alternative is to score the strictness of the various aspects of a country's regulatory apparatus, and combine these component scores into an overall ranking. One such approach was pioneered by Grubb and Wells (1993) for OECD countries. To give some idea of the basis for their calculations, Table 6 summarises certain aspects of labour market regulation in the major EU countries in the early 1990s. The US and Japan are included as well for comparative purposes. The table does not attempt to be exhaustive, presenting only the more striking regulations. Noteworthy is the high minimum wage in France, where the minimum is no less than 73 per cent of the manual manufacturing wage (column 1). By contrast, the corresponding US value is just 37 per cent. It can also be seen that many European countries severely limit the employer's freedom to dismiss permanent staff by requiring that the labour authorities be notified in advance, among other things (column 3). This limitation occurs in Greece, Italy, the Netherlands (which has since liberalised its law), Portugal, and Spain. Even where the notification is not required, laws giving works councils co-determination power over dismissals (as in Germany) may in practice act as a substantial barrier. Several countries also proscribe temporary work agencies (column 4).[20] In addition, as shown in the fifth column of the table, there are wide-ranging restrictions on hours. Ceilings on weekly hours and on overtime are common, as are bans on night work. In addition, most countries require at least four or five weeks paid holiday (column 6).

Rankings of the strictness of employment protection are given in Table 7. The first two columns show the results of two Commission employer surveys in 1989 and 1994, illustrating the direct approach to estimating regulatory strictness. The two surveys hardly correlate at all.[21] Given that the laws (and/or their application) are unlikely to have changed so radically, the low correlation probably indicates the difficulty employers must have had in interpreting the question. The two surveys do agree, however, that the UK is least strict.

The next two columns of Table 7 are based on assessments of the legal position.[22] While the OECD index aims to measure employment protection, the Grubb–Wells index is broader-based, relating to restrictions on overall employee work. In

---

[20] The various laws are in flux; for example, Spain relaxed its rules in 1993 to allow temporary work agencies that operate on a non-profit basis.

[21] The correlation coefficient (r) is 0.14.

[22] The OECD (1994, Tables 6.5 and 6.6) procedure evaluates countries' strictness of employment protection legislation as of the late 1980s. Variables included are: procedural inconveniences (for example, scale 0 to 3 for dismissal notice procedure, where 0 = simple written statement, and 3 = third party permission); days delay to start of notice; months of severance pay (for workers of 9 months, 4 years, and 20 years of service); and difficulty of dismissal (including definition of unfair dismissal, where 0 = worker capability or economic reasons are grounds for fair dismissal, and 3 = worker capability can never be grounds for dismissal). This exercise is performed for laws pertaining to two types of labour contract: regular contracts and fixed-term contracts. Countries are then ranked according to each of these indicators separately, and an overall ranking for the two types of contracts is constructed by taking the unweighted average of the separate rankings. Finally, the rankings for the two types of contract are averaged. (The Grubb–Wells index is similar, but rankings are added for restrictions on hours worked.)

Table 6: Summary of Labour Market Regulation (Early 1990s)

	Min. wage/ average manual wage ratio	Extension of collective agreements	Special protection for individual dismissals	Restrictions on temporary agencies	Special restrictions on hours	Statutory paid vacation (weeks)
Belgium	69	Frequent			Max. 39 hours/week; night work generally banned	4
Denmark	0	Frequent			Max. 39 hours/week; max. overtime 144 hours/yr	5
France	73	Frequent	Compensation up to 2 years pay		Max. 39 hours/week	5
Germany	0	Fairly frequent	Works council co-determines			3
Greece	57	Universal	Authorities to be notified	Illegal	Max. 40 hours/week; max. overtime 135 hours/year	4
Ireland	0	Rare				3
Italy	0	Universal	Authorities to be notified	Illegal until 1997		4
Nether-lands	60	Fairly frequent	Authorities to be notified		Nightwork generally banned	4
Portugal	70	Possible	Authorities to be notified			4.4
Spain	40	Rare	Authorities to be notified	Illegal until 1994	Max. 40 hours/week; max. overtime 80 hours/year	5
UK	0	None				No law
Japan	53	Rare				10-20 days
USA	37	None			Max. 40 hours/week*	No law

* with the exception of administrative and sales workers earning over given threshold.

Source: Siebert (1997), Tables 10.1-10.4.

Table 7: Ranking of Countries by Strictness of Labour Market Regulation

	Employer survey on hiring and firing laws as obstacle to employing more people		OECD index of stringency of employment protection laws[c]	Grubb-Wells index of restrictions on overall employee work[d]
	(% answering 'very important')		(point score)	(ranking)
	1989[a]	1994[b]		
Belgium	27	29	10.50	5
Denmark	n.a.	n.a.	3.25	2
France	32	26	9.50	6
Germany	21	29	12.00	7
Greece	27	19	11.00	10
Ireland	29	30	2.75	3
Italy	45	14	14.25	8
Netherlands	44	21	7.25	4
Portugal	29	20	12.50	11
Spain	35	38	11.25	9
UK	9	11	2.25	1
Japan	—	—	3.71	—
US	—	—	0.36	—

Note: The lower the score, for both the OECD and the Grubb-Wells indices, the less strict is labour market regulation. The rank correlation between the OECD index and the Grubb-Wells index is 0.90 (p<0.001); that between the OECD index and the EU 1989 employer index is 0.46 (p<0.19).

Sources: [a] Commission (1991); [b] Commission (1995c); [c] OECD (1994), Table 6.7; [d] Grubb and Wells (1993).

particular, it includes limitations on hours of work. In fact, the (rank) correlation between these two indices is high (r = 0.90). Admittedly, a problem with the legal definition of employment protection is that it ignores variability in the enforcement of law and other idiosyncrasies. Thus, for example, the table shows that the Portuguese labour market is among the most heavily regulated. Portuguese law in the 1980s, for example, did not permit worker capability to be grounds for dismissal (see OECD, 1994, Table 6.5). Yet Portuguese firms were apparently able in part to avoid this law by building up pay 'arrears' (not paying) for workers whose services were no longer required. Nevertheless, as shown below, the law-based measures of employment protection provide plausible results.

The Effects of Employment Protection

Broad Associations: It is interesting initially to consider some simple relationships between economic performance and regulation. Take, *first,* the association between private sector employment growth *per capita* 1979-90 (OECD, 1994, Table 1.1), and the Grubb–Wells index of regulation. The more regulated countries tend to have slower private sector employment growth.[23] It is worth noting that the UK was the only member state of the EU to have positive private sector employment growth over the 1979-90 period.

A *second* interesting relationship is that between the ratio of youth to adult unemployment (as given in OECD, 1994, Table 1.17) and the Grubb–Wells index of regulation. The more regulated countries clearly have relatively more youth unemployment.[24] Many factors affect unemployment, including expenditures on unemployment benefits and on training programmes, but these factors will affect both youths and adults. Taking the ratio helps net such common factors out. The fact that youths do worse in the labour markets of the more regulated countries implies that regulation helps 'insiders' (established workers already in jobs) who cannot easily be fired. The job opportunities of younger workers are thereby limited.

Third, there is a link between temporary employment contracts (as given in Grubb and Wells, 1993, Table 4) and the Grubb–Wells index. The more regulated a country, the higher its proportion of temporary workers.[25] The reason for this

---

[23] The rank correlation is $r = -0.463$, which is statistically significant at the 13 per cent level ($p < 0.13$): $p < 0.13$ means that there is a less than a 13 per cent chance of being wrong in rejecting the null hypothesis that the correlation is zero.

[24] The rank correlation is $r = 0.626$ ($p < 0.03$).

[25] $r = 0.730$ ($p < 0.01$).

association is presumably that temporary workers have less employment protection, and are also in many instances less costly to employ because of lower fringe benefits such as holiday entitlements. A way of 'contracting around' the labour regulations is therefore to hire temporary workers. The implication is that laws which aim to make employment more stable can have the opposite effect.

Multivariate Analysis: Simple correlations such as these are suggestive, but there is always the possibility that an unmeasured third factor is causing the relationship. A properly specified model is required, taking into account a much wider set of factors than regulation alone.

A well-known multivariate study is that of Lazear (1990), who examines the effect of severance pay on employment and unemployment in 20 nations over the interval 1954-86. The stringency of dismissals protection is measured by the severance pay entitlement of a blue-collar worker with 10 years' service, dismissed because of inadequate labour demand. (Note that these are rules covering individual rather than collective redundancies; regulations covering the latter differ so widely across nations as to preclude any consistent measure.) Lazear finds that the more generous the severance pay entitlement, the lower the employment-population ratio and the labour force participation rate, and the higher the unemployment rate.

Lazear's study has occasioned no small controversy, partly because of its use of just one measure of employment protection and, more important, because of data problems and the parsimonious nature of his estimating equations (see Addison and Grosso, 1996). Interesting studies by Scarpetta (1996) and Nickell (1997) have widened the measure of employment protection somewhat and deployed a much more extensive set of controls to narrow the omitted variables problem. In the process, however, they have had to forgo charting changes in employment protection through time, as did Lazear.

Scarpetta's 17-country study, covering the period 1983-93, considers the impact of employment protection on four outcome measures: the overall unemployment rate, the youth unemployment rate, the long-term unemployment rate, and the non-employment rate (the unemployed plus the economically inactive as a proportion of the working-age population). His measure of employment protection is the OECD index given in the third column of Table 7. Nickell constructs a similar model, but does not consider the important youth unemployment variable. Each of the outcome variables is given a long list of determinants, as shown in Table 8.

Both Scarpetta and Nickell find that in the main the determinants of joblessness have the effects we would expect. As Table 8 shows, employment protection legislation is positively associated with total unemployment rates (though Nickell does not find this), youth unemployment rates, long-term unemployment rates, and non-employment rates, holding all other factors constant. The strength of the link depends upon equation specification, but is positive and significant in most specifications. The impact on youth unemployment reported by Scarpetta is particularly marked, with an estimated elasticity of between 0.52 and 1.04. In other words, the estimated effect of a 10 per cent increase in the employment protection index is a 5.2 per cent to 10.4 per cent increase in the youth unemployment rate. For total unemployment the elasticity is considerably smaller, 0.08 to 0.33. As we have noted, Nickell finds no overall unemployment effect.

Employment protection laws are thus found to have a stronger impact on youth and on long-term unemployment than on total unemployment. This disparity has important distributional implications. It supports the view that such legislation helps the insider groups. Adults, for example, tend to be insiders compared to youth. The young and the disadvantaged (who are the long-term unemployed) suffer to help the rest.

Nickell also contrasts the effects of employment protection laws on the non-employment rate for the population as a whole, and for prime-age males (those aged 25-54 years). Employment protection laws increase overall non-employment, as can be seen from the table. However, Nickell emphasises that this effect does not carry through to prime-age males (in an equation not summarised in Table 8). He interprets this contrast not as a general 'insider' phenomenon but, rather, as a reflection of the low participation rates of females in southern Europe that

61

Table 8: Determinants of Joblessness – Results from Scarpetta (1996) and Nickell (1997)

Sign and significance of coefficients (elasticity in parentheses)

		Total unemployment rate % [mean 8.41%]	Youth unemployment rate (16-24) [mean 16.6%]	Long-term unemployment rate [mean 3.5%]	Non-employment rate [mean 35.6%]
Employment Protection Index [mean 7.14]	Scarpetta	Generally positive and significant (0.08–0.33)	Positive and significant (0.52–1.04)	Generally positive and significant (0.24 –1.0)	Positive and significant (0.15–0.31)
	Nickell	Insignificant	n.a.	Positive and significant	Positive and significant
Unemployment Benefit Replacement Rate [mean total 31.5%, youth 55.0%, LTU 19.0%]	Scarpetta	Positive and significant (0.49)	Positive and significant (0.50–0.60)	Tends to be insignificant	Insignificant
	Nickell	Positive and significant	n.a.	Positive and significant	Insignificant
Unionisation [mean 38.2%]	Scarpetta	Generally positive and significant (0.45)	Positive and significant (0.46–0.74)	Generally positive and significant (0.33– 0.76)	Positive and significant (0.09–0.15)
	Nickell	Positive and significant	n.a.	Positive and significant	Insignificant

Table 8 (cont'd.)

Tax Wedge [mean 41.1%]	Scarpetta	Insignificant	Insignificant	Positive and significant (1.17)	Insignificant
	Nickell	Positive and significant	n.a.	Positive and significant	Positive and significant
Active labour market exps. per person unemployed relative to GNP *per capita* [mean 22.0%]	Scarpetta	Insignificant	Insignificant	Insignificant	Tends to be insignificant
	Nickell	Negative and significant	n.a.	Negative and significant	Insignificant

Note. The top left cell, for example, shows that the employment protection index has a generally positive and significant effect (depending upon equation specification) on total unemployment. Elasticity figure means that a 10% increase in the employment protection index is associated with a 0.8% to 3.3% change in the total unemployment rate. Scarpetta's equations are fitted to data for 17 OECD countries over the 1983-93 period. (The means are taken across the whole sample for this period.) In addition to the listed variables, there are controls for the GDP output gap (gap between actual and trend GDP), inter-firm and inter-union 'co-ordination of bargaining', an index of exposure to foreign competition, an index of trade restrictions, an average of real long-term interest rates, and a terms-of-trade variable.

Nickell's equations are fitted to data for 20 OECD countries for averages of two time periods, 1983-88 and 1989-94. Controls include, in addition to the listed variables: unemployment benefit duration, union coverage, inter-firm and inter-union co-ordination of bargaining, change in inflation, and a dummy for 1989-94.

Sources: Scarpetta (1996); Nickell (1997).

happens to coincide with strong employment protection because of a culture which places weight on the position of the male head of household. His argument seems to be stretching the evidence.

In addition, Table 8 reveals that joblessness tends to be positively associated with the level of unemployment benefits, with unionisation, and with the tax wedge. The unemployment benefit effect is to be expected, though it is quite small: a 10 per cent increase in the replacement rate increases the contemporaneous unemployment rate by 4.9 per cent. In the UK case, because most of the changes in the unemployment rate are caused by changes in duration, this would amount to about an extra 1.5 weeks unemployment given an average duration of seven or eight months.[26] For its part, the union-isation effect on unemployment is presumably caused by the greater real wage rigidity associated with unions (Scarpetta, 1996, p. 64). Interestingly, both Scarpetta (1996, p. 71) and Nickell (1997, p. 68) find that co-ordination of collective bargaining helps reduce unemployment, so the adverse effects of unions do not appear inevitable. On the other hand, the offset is indirect. The key element is employer co-ordination.[27] The union effect is more marked for youth unemployment: the unionisation elasticity ranges from 0.46 to 0.74. The adverse impact of unions on youth unemployment again implies that when insiders are strong (as reflected in high union density), wages are set above market-clearing levels for junior workers.[28]

---

[26] These values pertain to the 1980s; see Layard *et al.* (1991, p. 224).

[27] Horst Siebert (1997, p. 47), also cautions that these results are unlikely to survive the 1990s, and that centralisation *per se* hinders the necessary dispersion of the wage structure.

[28] As for the tax wedge, this consists of payroll, income and consumption taxes which open up a wedge between take-home wages and the cost of labour to the firm. Basic economic analysis predicts that increased taxes will simply cause take-home wages to fall, leaving unemployment unaffected. It has to be assumed that wages are flexible downwards (ignoring minimum wage and unemployment benefit floors), and the labour reallocation necessitated by taxing this and subsidising that occurs quickly. These assumptions are strong and appear to be refuted empirically. Thus, as can be seen, Nickell finds an increased tax wedge to raise unemployment, as does Scarpetta in the case of long-term unemployment. In practice, taxes are not good for jobs.

As a final word on Table 8, we see that Nickell and Scarpetta differ somewhat with regard to the impact of 'active labour market policy', that is, training expenditures on unemployment. Scarpetta finds insignificant effects for all outcomes, while Nickell finds active policies to be helpful for unemployment, but not for employment. We would stress the employment results here, since unemployment figures might tend to be massaged downwards for cosmetic reasons by training programmes. The lack of a positive employment effect of government training programmes is of course inconsistent with the 'externalities' argument that there should be intervention in the training market – or at least indicates that training programmes have not been successful in combating such externalities.

A recent study by Morton and Siebert (1997) also reports evidence of adverse impacts of regulation for unskilled workers. The authors compare 10 matched plants in the UK and continental Europe. Five multinationals are involved; the countries considered in the study are the UK, Germany, France, Belgium, and the Netherlands. The focus is not on employment protection, but more generally on less-regulated versus more-regulated economies.

Data from the study are summarised in Table 9. Although the comparison involves plants producing identical products, the UK plants operate very differently from their continental European counterparts. Overtime hours are higher in the UK, and holidays are shorter, reflecting the lack of regulation. Quit rates are also higher in the UK, which can presumably be attributed to less favourable wages and working conditions.[29] Moreover, dismissals are considerably higher in the UK, again presumably the result of lesser employment protection. The higher dismissal risk might also make worker supervision easier, which in turn could be a factor explaining the lower absence rates of UK plants.

As can also be seen, total labour costs are about 60 per cent higher in the continental European plants. Competition requires that such higher costs be matched by higher labour productivity. As measured, the continental European plants indeed have about a 40 per cent advantage in this respect.

---

[29] Lower UK unemployment – to the extent that this obtains – might also be a factor.

Table 9: UK-Europe Plant Comparisons

	Average for UK plants	Average for continental European plants
Overtime hours per year	170.0**	23.4
Days holiday per year	25.8**	35.4
Quit rate (% per year)	2.5 to 3.2***	0.9
Dismissal rate (% per year)	0.9***	0.3
Absenteeism (hours per worker per year)	75.8**	129.8
Gross pay	£19,900	£23,150
Total labour cost	£23,400**	£35,800
Labour productivity, ratio European plants/UK plants	1.40	
Proportion of plant workforce temporary, part-time or guest-worker	8.4%*	20.8%
Proportion of plant workforce with less than 1 year's experience	8.4%*	2.7%
Proportion of plant workforce aged more than 55 years	16.0%***	5.8%

Notes: ***, **, * denote significance of difference in means at the 1%, 5% and 10% levels, respectively.

Data are from workforces of matched plants of five multinationals producing the same product (e.g. engines or margarine) in the UK and continental Europe.

Source: Morton and Siebert (1997).

Accompanying higher labour productivity, we would expect tighter hiring standards, implying that employment is not offered, say, to the inexperienced young worker or to the much older worker. Table 9 shows this to be the case. The continental European plants have a smaller proportion of workers with under one year's experience (2.7 per cent) than their UK counterparts (8.4 per cent). Similarly, the continental European plants employ a smaller proportion of older workers, aged over 55 years (5.8 per cent), than their UK counterparts (16.0 per cent). On this evidence, continental European plants exhibit a reduced demand for unskilled workers (the young, the inexperienced, and those at the end of their careers), and they also tend to substitute temporary for permanent workers. The implication is that the high labour costs associated with regulated labour markets damage the less well-off.

The negative consequences of employment protection for employment receive support from a number of US studies. In particular, analyses of the erosion of the common law employment-at-will principle point to fairly sharply reduced employment. Thus, for example, Dertouzos and Karoly (1993), using state-level data for the period 1980-89, find that employment is 3 per cent lower, *ceteris paribus*, in the years following a state's recognition of tort damages for wrongful dismissal.[30] (In determining employment, they hold constant state output, allow for state and year fixed effects, and control for the endogeneity of regulation.) On this analysis, employment protection costs firms more than it benefits workers: in terms of Figure 2, point C is to the left of point B. And in a separate study of workers' compensation insurance (see below), Kaestner (1996) reports that employment is systematically lower, the higher are employers' costs.

Some Contrary Evidence

Influential economists such as Stephen Nickell (1996, 1997) of Oxford and Richard Freeman (see, in particular, Blank and Freeman, 1994) of Harvard are sceptical of the largely negative evidence assembled here.

One of Nickell's main points (1997, p. 57) is that the UK's unemployment rate, which averaged 9.7 per cent over 1983-96, is higher than that of many of its European neighbours, even if its labour market is the most flexible. To the reply that UK unemployment might be yet higher were it not for such flexibility, Nickell would presumably counter that his

---

[30] It is only fair to point out that Dertouzos and Karoly speculate that the benefits of unjust dismissals legislation might be worth the costs.

econometric analysis does not reveal much of a link between employment protection laws and total unemployment. Moreover, Nickell has argued (Nickell and Bell, 1996, p. 303) that Britain's unemployment record for unskilled workers is worse than that of West Germany, even though unskilled workers' pay relative to skilled pay has fallen much more in the UK (he stresses the way the German apprenticeship system helps the unskilled).

Information on inequalities in unemployment according to education is given in Table 10. It can be seen that less educated workers generally have higher unemployment rates than their more educated counterparts. The simplest explanation for such inequality is that less educated workers command lower wages – which are closer to wage floors set by minimum wage laws and unemployment benefits. (Labour markets for less educated workers might also have experienced more turbulence due to biased technological change, and to Third World competition.) Special factors must explain the strange reversal of the norm in Italy in 1979, and for Japanese women. We can by-pass accounting for such factors by considering trends. Data for 1979-94 are also given in Table 10. It can be seen that in the UK there is no trend: the ratio has remained quite steady both for men (about 2.5) and women (1.4–1.6). In Japan there is also no obvious trend. However, in the regulated markets of France, Germany and Italy the position of the less educated has deteriorated. Admittedly, the US also shows a trend against the less educated, and this would seem to upset any simple equation of employment regulation with insider power. Nevertheless, contrary to Nickell, it does appear that the unregulated UK has maintained the job opportunities of the unskilled better than its major competitor countries in the EU. This conclusion is supported by the trends in employment-population ratios shown in Table 5 (above, p. 55) which point to a reasonable UK job creation performance.

Blank and Freeman (1994) have also questioned the link between labour regulation and unemployment. In the first place, they point out that although many European countries increased labour market flexibility and reduced state involvement and transfer programmes during the 1980s, this was not accompanied by any reduction in unemployment.

It is difficult to know for certain how employment

Table 10: Unemployment by Education, Adults 25-55

		Unemployment rate by education, 1994 (%)		Ratio, lower to upper education:			Public expenditures as % of GDP (average 1992/3 and 1995/6)	
		Lower secondary or less	Upper secondary or more	1994	1990	1979	Active labour market policies[a]	Unemployment compensation
France:	men	14	8	1.8	2.0	1.4	1.2	1.9
	women	16	10	1.6	1.8	1.3		
Germany:	men	15	6	2.5	2.9	2.3	1.5	2.5
	women	13	9	1.4	1.5	1.2		
Italy:	men	6	5	1.2	1.0	0.5	0.8	1.0[b]
	women	13	10	1.3	1.1	0.9		
Netherlands:	men	7	4	1.8	2.0	2.2	1.4	3.0
	women	10	5	2.0	-	-		
UK[c]:	men	19	8	2.4	2.6	2.5	0.6	1.5
	women	8	5	1.6	1.6	1.4		
Japan:	men	3	2	-	1.5[d]	1.9	0.1	0.3
	women	7	9	-	0.8[d]	0.8		
US:	men	13	5	2.6	2.5	2.1	0.2	0.4
	women	12	5	2.4	2.4	2.0		

[a] Active labour market policies include expenditures on the public employment service, adult training programmes, youth training, subsidised employment, and measures for the disabled.

[b] Italian unemployment compensation expenditure average is over 1991 and 1992.

[c] Note that a major change in the UK definition of unemployment took place after 1979, so that the results for 1979 and 1990 are not strictly comparable, especially for levels.

[d] Unemployment figure relates to 1992.

Sources: OECD (1994), Table 1.16; OECD (1997), Tables D and K.

protection changed over the 1980s. Abstracting from Lazear's study, the favoured indices of employment protection relate to the late 1980s, and there are no parallel data for the early 1980s. But it is certainly not true, for example, that transfers in the form of unemployment assistance declined in the 1980s for major European countries.[31] Admittedly, some countries have attempted to reduce labour regulation, but it might reasonably be argued that these changes have been too marginal to have had much effect. Thus, Horst Siebert (1997, p. 41) has characterised the 1985 changes in dismissal protection, social plans, and access to temporary employment contracts realised under the German Employment Promotion Act as 'minor'. Equally, the 1987 changes in French law relaxing the constraint that the labour authorities be consulted over all collective layoffs have to be viewed as modest because of the low employment threshold involved. We do not find it surprising, therefore, that a number of observers have failed to detect any corresponding improvement in the sluggish speed of employment adjustment in these two countries (see, for example, Abraham and Houseman, 1994).

In the second place, Blank and Freeman (1994) stress the need to evaluate the benefits side of the labour market regulation coin. For example, dismissals protection laws insure against job instability, and the value of this protection has somehow to be set against any labour market inflexibilities that are caused.

While it might seem almost impossible to measure benefits, our earlier discussion (again refer to Figure 2) has made it clear that employment will rise if the costs of a mandate are less than the benefits as evaluated by workers. The employment effects of mandates – which we have been emphasising all along – therefore provide a simple test of this argument. The information supplied in Tables 8 and 9 provides signs that the employment (and distributional) effects of employment protection regulation are likely to be negative, with the

---

[31] For OECD European countries as a whole, the OECD summary measure of the gross unemployment benefit replacement rate, excluding housing benefit, grew considerably: from 14 per cent in 1961 to 25 per cent in 1979 to 34 per cent in 1995 – see Martin (1996, p. 103).

inference that the benefits of such regulation are less than the costs.

Lessons from a Flexible Wage Economy

The most convincing empirical studies of mandates use US state data. All 50 states can be followed over time as the mandates change. Because the states have variation in the strength of their mandates, it is possible to perform a simultaneous cross-state and cross-time analysis, which allows more variables to be kept constant.

Workers' Compensation: Studies of workers' compensation for accidents also provide evidence on the wages and employment effects of mandates. Workers' compensation is intended to provide an alternative to court actions for damages for workplace injury. Such litigation is expensive and uncertain. Workers' compensation laws require firms to offer guaranteed no-fault accident compensation according to an agreed schedule (making the damages limited but certain). The British mandate was the first, dating from 1897 when it required employers to pay a £300 lump sum for a workplace death, and 50 per cent of previous weekly earnings for total or partial incapacity (see Bartrip, 1987). Most US states introduced similar mandates between 1910 and 1923. Using data from this period, Fishback and Kantor (1995) demonstrate that wages tended to fall in their sample industries with the introduction of workers' compensation. The fall in wages was approximately the same as the rise in expected post-accident compensation, suggesting that the value of the scheme to workers equalled its cost to employers. Full wage offsets in response to more generous workers' compensation are also suggested in results using US state data for the 1970s and 1980s (see Moore and Viscusi, 1990).

Robert Kaestner (1996) has also examined the effects of workers' compensation in a study which is particularly interesting because it analyses both wage and employment consequences. His results can be directly interpreted in the framework of Figure 2. He uses US state data, 1982-89, for young men, and contrasts the effects of workers' compensation with two other mandates, namely, unemployment insurance and minimum wages. The results are summarised in Table 11.

71

Taking the 16-19-year-old group first, we see that all three mandates have statistically significant negative effects on labour-force participation (LFP). Given that population is already controlled for in the regression, the negative coefficient points to a negative employment effect of the mandates. As for wage effects, neither changes in workers' compensation nor in unemployment insurance payments affect the wage. This is to be expected, since the wage of the youngest men is close to the minimum wage floor. The importance of the minimum wage is shown by the high elasticity of the 16-19-year-old group's wage with respect to the minimum wage (0.5).

The older groups exhibit less employment sensitivity to workers' compensation and to unemployment insurance. This is also to be expected, because older workers are more likely to be insiders and their wages are less constrained by minimum wage floors. Notice, however, that these groups still exhibit significant negative employment effects due to workers' compensation. Admittedly, there are also some rather odd findings. Although wages are negatively associated with workers' compensation – which chimes in well with the negative employment effect – the wage effect tends to be too great.[32] The positive effect of unemployment insurance on wages for the 25-34 group (elasticity 0.3) is also puzzling.

Nevertheless, the overall picture painted in Table 11 is reasonably consistent. The negative employment effects are accompanied by negative wage effects. The picture is one of downward shifts of both the supply and demand curves, the demand shift being greater, implying employer costs outweigh worker benefits. The fact that negative employment effects are weaker for the older groups is consistent both with their being insiders, and with their greater potential wage flexibility – that is, minimum wages are less binding.

---

[32] The elasticity of –0.12 for the 20-24 group implies that a 10 per cent rise in the employer's workers' compensation contribution (measured as a proportion of the wage bill) is associated with a 1.2 per cent fall in the wage. But in Kaestner's dataset workers' compensation contributions average only about 1.5 per cent of the wage bill. A rise of 10 per cent in the contribution ratio would therefore cost 0.15 per cent of the wage bill but result in wage savings amounting to 1.2 per cent of the wage bill. This is evidently too much.

Table 11: Wage and Employment Effects of Mandates - Summary Results from Kaestner's (1996) Study

Sign and significance of coefficients (elasticity in parentheses)

Mandate	16-19 year olds		20-24 year olds		25-34 year olds	
	Labour-force participation	Wage	Labour-force participation	Wage	Labour-Force Participation	Wage
Workers' compensation	Negative and significant (- 0.05)	Insignificant	Negative and significant (- 0.04)	Negative and significant (- 0.12)	Negative and significant (- 0.02)	Negative and significant (- 0.06)
Unemployment insurance	Negative and significant (- 0.03)	Insignificant	Insignificant	Insignificant	Insignificant	Positive and significant (0.03)
Minimum wage	Negative and significant (- 0.14)	Positive and significant (0.5)	Negative and significant (- 0.02)	Positive and significant (0.4)	Insignificant	Positive and significant (0.2)

Note: The top left cell for example shows that states and time periods with higher workers' compensation premium payments have lower labourforce participation for youths in the 16-19 age group, other things equal. Here, a 10% increase in workers' compensation means a 0.5% decrease in labourforce participation.

The equations are fitted to data for the 50 US states and the District of Columbia for the period 1982-1989, giving 408 datapoints. Other variables controlled are the percentage of population in the relevant age group, and the male unemployment rate.

Source: Kaestner (1996), Tables 3-8; authors' calculations.

73

Maternity Benefits: Let us finally briefly consider the case of mandated maternity benefits. Some pointed results have again been presented using US state data (Gruber, 1994). The research here is related to the requirement in some US states to extend company health insurance plans to include maternity expenditures. Gruber's results indicate that in the affected states the mandate raised firms' annual insurance premiums by about 5 per cent of the weekly wage of women aged 20-40 years. At the same time, the weekly wages of such women fell by about 5 per cent. There were only minor employment and hours effects – including an increase in hours worked suggesting that some part-timers were displaced. In terms of Figure 2, it looks as though this mandate simply did not help women much (the notional point C lying vertically below point B). Thus most if not all of the costs of the US maternity insurance mandate were shifted on to the workers, with the part-timers losing out.

Summary: In sum, while for a variety of statistical reasons we have little confidence in the point estimates contained in the various studies reviewed here, the net effect of employment protection and analogous rules on labour demand (and supply) does seem to be lower employment, greater and longer unemployment for some, and, implicitly, a decline in the speed with which labour relocates from declining to growing sectors of the economy. To this extent, the favourable employment and unemployment development in the US would appear to owe more than a little to its lower (but by no means negligible) degree of employment protection.[33]

Acceptance of this conclusion does not of course imply that all employment regulations have the same effect, even if it is undoubtedly the case that some are reinforcing (as when limitations on the employer's ability to lay off labour will be intensified if firms cannot adjust along the margins of wages and hours because of minimum wage and hours restrictions). Nor would we wish to imply that the trade-offs are invariant as between countries. Rather, we are summarising the necessarily

---

[33] For an interesting, and in our view thoroughly complementary, diagnosis of the source of the US competitive edge in employment creation which emphasises that country's greater 'entrepreneurialism', see Krueger and Pischke (1997).

broad implications of the cross-country analyses. Precision awaits properly parametrised models at individual country level. It would be idle to pretend otherwise. But the broad conclusion is nevertheless that the upward harmonisation sought by the Commission confronts potentially serious costs in the form of disemployment and reduced employment growth.

Mandates may often cost more than they benefit. They assuredly require wage flexibility not characteristic of Europe. State-of-the-art studies such as those we have summarised should form the basis of investigations of the cost of mandates.

V. Conclusions

We have traced the development of social policy in the European Union from its origins in the early 1970s. The employment, industrial relations, and social affairs directorate of the Commission has been shown to have been single minded in its pursuit of pan-European rules. It has seen off its principal antagonists, and its dogged persistence – witness the long history of much current EU legislation and the precursors of the Commission's current proposals – has paid off in that most of its policy agenda has been enacted into law. It now stands at the peak of its regulatory power/authority, and will push harder if the economic aggregates prove obliging. And the importance of the employment chapter should not be lost sight of at a time when monetary union might otherwise be expected to impart a sharp deregulatory thrust to the Union.

At issue is the efficacy and impact of European social policy. There are many who view the mass of labour market directives as either benign or as a small price to pay for economic integration. Then there are those who believe the European endeavour is as much involved with social as economic issues, and who accordingly take a positive view of the social chapter and its antecedents, even to the extent of arguing that social union facilitates economic union.

Interestingly, proponents of these views have offered almost no supportive economic analysis. Certainly, the Commission, although charged with evaluating the possible effects of its measures on the labour market in general and upon small- and medium-sized firms in particular, via so-called '*fiches d'impact*', has failed to meet this obligation. It has neither the resources nor, let us be frank, the will to do so.

It has seldom given its proposals an economic efficiency basis, and then only in muddled terms having to do with distortions of competition and social dumping. Rather, its emphasis has been on ethereal notions of fundamental social rights, that is, upon equity considerations. But economic

76

analysis is called for even if the goal of achieving a European 'social space' is not at root efficiency based. *Faute de mieux*, we have had to put the Commission's case for it. We have shown among other things that the issues raised by the possibility of market failure are real, and have to be confronted. Hence blanket rejection of labour market mandates is unproductive. By the same token, we have also shown that the general issue of government failure must always be borne in mind.

A fundamental critique of European social policy would be the sheer amateurishness of the entire endeavour, partly indexed by the web of overlapping and even inconsistent legislation. The near analytical vacuum in which policy discussion is framed is a cause for concern. Whatever the record of the past, it is assuredly dangerous for Europe to embark on the next stage of social policy with an unreformed set of procedures in Brussels.

But before we turn to the issue of institutional reform, there is the important question of the labour market impact of the social charter/chapter experiments. The facts of the matter are that it is too soon to tell given the vintage of the measures and the spotty record of implementation at member-state level. We are after all only just now observing the pay-offs to Mrs Thatcher's labour market reform agenda in the UK – a framework seemingly largely accepted by Mr Blair – and also perhaps the teleological consequences of the era of 'cosy corporatism' in post-war Germany (see Soltwedel, 1997). What we have been able to show is that measures analogous to those proposed by the Commission have associated disemployment and unemployment consequences, a finding which undermines the basis of upward harmonisation of labour standards. Importantly, in view of the equity rationale for policy, such evidence is strongest for the less skilled groups in society.

If press reports are to be believed, the Commission seems to have been more than a little sensitive to the empirical evidence, even to the extent of suppressing it in official publications (see *Financial Times*, 1996). To be sure, the results of the econometric analyses on which we have drawn are mixed, indirect and potentially consistent with individual countries bucking the trend as a result of potential trade-offs available at the national level (see Paqué, 1997). But even this latter possibility manifestly fails to provide an economic rationale for pan-European rules; indeed, it only serves to underline the importance of subsidiarity.

In the light of the above, one important policy recommendation would be that Europe should recognise that social policy cannot be practised in a vacuum, or for that matter conducted on what might, however inelegantly, be termed a suck-it-and-see basis, since the record confirms that the Commission's mandates have always been revised in one direction only – upward. Specifically, the time has come to subject Commission proposals to a form of efficiency audit. The intention should not be to prevent the development of social policy but rather to present the Council, the European Parliament, and other European entities, as well as the public, with information on the financial impact of new mandates and their likely disemployment and other consequences. Ideally, the DG-V should not be expected to assume this function or to be responsible for commissioning studies to this end. One possibility is for an independent function akin to that assumed by the Congressional Budget Office (CBO) in the US, under the Unfunded Mandates Reform Act of 1995, although this may not go far enough.[34]

In any event, the EU bureaucracy has agencies other than DG-V well suited to an investigative role (for example, the competition directorate). As we are often told, Europe may indeed choose to follow a social path different from that of the United States (or Japan), but this desire should not remove the need to evaluate each and every mandate. As a policy recommendation, this will only be regarded as radical/subversive by those whose producer group interests dominate

---

[34] The CBO is charged with estimating the cost of inter-governmental, federal mandates. When these estimated costs exceed $50 million annually, any member of the House or Senate can raise a point of order on any bill and, unless waived by a majority vote, the bill dies. The CBO is also directed to estimate whether a mandate that binds the private sector exceeds $100 million annually, although in this case no point of order is triggered if the cost exceeds this threshold. Currently, draft legislation before the US Senate seeks to put inter-governmental mandates and private-sector mandates on the same footing.

in discussions over the shape of Europe's social space. If, as we suspect, Mr Blair does see the social dimension of the European Union as a side-show, there is every indication that he is mistaken. We have argued that the strait-jacket of ever-wider EU regulations will disadvantage member states in general, and Britain in particular given its very different institutional arrangements and voluntaristic tradition.

References

Abraham, Katherine, and Susan Houseman (1994): 'Does Employment Protection Inhibit Labor Market Flexibility?: Lessons from Germany, France and Belgium', in Rebecca Blank (ed.), *Social Protection Versus Economic Flexibility – Is There a Trade-Off?*, Chicago: University of Chicago Press, pp. 59-93.

Addison, John T., and Jean-Luc Grosso (1996): 'Job Security Provisions and Employment: Revised Estimates,' *Industrial Relations*, Vol. 35 (October), pp. 585-603.

Addison, John T., and W. Stanley Siebert (1993): *Social Engineering in the European Community: The Social Charter, Maastricht and Beyond*, Current Controversies No. 6, London: Institute of Economic Affairs.

Addison, John T., and W. Stanley Siebert (1994): 'Vocational Training in the European Community', *Oxford Economic Papers*, Vol. 46 (October), pp. 696-724.

Addison, John T., and W. Stanley Siebert (1997): *Labour Markets in Europe: Issues of Harmonization and Regulation*, London: The Dryden Press.

Addison, John T., Richard Barrett, and W. Stanley Siebert (1998): 'Mandated Benefits and Firm Heterogeneity', (unpublished paper), University of Birmingham Department of Commerce (September).

Bartrip, Peter (1987): *Workmen's Compensation in the 20th Century*, Aldershot: Avebury.

Becker, Gary (1964) (1975, 2nd edn.): *Human Capital: A Theoretical and Empirical Analysis*, New York: Columbia University Press for National Bureau of Economic Research.

Blank, Rebecca, and Richard Freeman (1994): 'Evaluating the Connection between Social Protection and Economic

Flexibility', in Rebecca Blank (ed.), *Social Protection Versus Economic Flexibility – Is There a Trade-Off?*, Chicago: University of Chicago Press, pp. 21-41.

Boal, William, and Michael Ransom (1997): 'Monopsony in the Labor Market', *Journal of Economic Literature*, Vol. 35 (March), pp. 86-112.

Burgess, Simon, and Hedley Rees (1996): 'Job Tenure in Britain 1975-92', *Economic Journal*, Vol. 106 (March), pp. 334-44.

Commission (1974): 'Social Action Programme', *Bulletin of the European Communities*, Supplement 2/74: 11-16, Brussels: Commission of the European Communities (CEC).

Commission (1989a): *Community Charter of the Fundamental Social Rights of Workers*, COM(89) 471 final, Brussels: CEC.

Commission (1989b): *Communication from the Commission Concerning Its Action Programme Relating to the Implementation of the Community Charter of Basic Social Rights of Workers*, COM(89) 568 final, Brussels: CEC.

Commission (1991): 'Developments in the Labour Market of the Community: Results of A Survey Covering Employers and Employees', *European Economy*, Vol. 47 (March).

Commission (1992): *From the Single Act to Maastricht and Beyond – the Means to Match our Ambitions*, COM(92) 2000 final, Brussels: CEC.

Commission (1993): *Growth Competitiveness, Employment – The Challenges and Ways Forward into the 21st Century*, COM(93) 700 final, Brussels: CEC.

Commission (1994): *European Social Policy – A Way Forward for the Union*, COM(94) 333, Brussels: CEC.

Commission (1995a): *Medium-Term Social Action Programme 1995-97*, COM(95) 134, Brussels: CEC.

Commission (1995b): *Commission Communication on Employee Information and Consultation*, COM(95) 547 final, Brussels: CEC, 14 November.

Commission (1995c): 'Performance of the European Labour Market: Results of an Ad Hoc Survey Covering Employers and Employees', *European Economy, Reports and Studies No. 3.*

Commission (1997a): *Commission Draft for the Joint Employment Report 1997* (Rev. 8), Brussels: CEC, 30 September.

Commission (1997b): *Commission Communication: Proposal for Guidelines for Member States Employment Policies 1998*, COM(97) 497 final, Brussels: CEC, 1 October.

Commission (1997c): *Commission Communication Concerning Information and Consultation of Employees within the National Framework – Consultative Document Addressed to the Social Partners at Community Level*, SEC(97), 1033 final, Brussels: CEC, 4 June.

Commission (1997d): *Commission Communication: Information and Consultation of Workers within the National Framework – Second Phase of Consultation of the Social Partners*, SEC(97) 2045 final, Brussels: CEC, 5 November.

Commission (1997e): *White Paper on Sectors and Activities Excluded from the Working Time Directive*, COM(97) 334 final, Brussels: CEC, 15 July.

Commission (1997f): *Green Paper on Partnership for a New Organisation of Work*, COM(97) 128 final, Brussels: CEC, 16 April.

Commission (1998): *Social Action Programme 1998-2000*, COM(98) 259, Brussels: CEC, 24 April.

Davignon (1997): *European Systems of Worker Involvement (with Regard to the European Company Statute and Other Pending Proposals), Final Report*, Brussels, May.

Dertouzos, James N., and Lynn A. Karoly (1993): 'Employment Effects of Worker Protection: Evidence from the United States.' In Christoph F. Buechtemann (ed.), *Employment Security and Labor Market Behavior – Interdisciplinary Approaches and International Evidence*, Ithaca, New York: ILR Press, pp. 215-27.

EIRR (1993): 'Maastricht and Social Policy – Part Two', *European Industrial Relations Review*, Vol. 239 (December), pp. 19-24.

EIRR (1997): 'No Agreement on Sexual Harassment', *European Industrial Relations Review*, Vol. 284 (September) p. 3.

EIRR (1998a): 'An Interview with Padraig Flynn', *European Industrial Relations Review*, Vol. 288 (January), pp. 20-23.

EIRR (1998b): 'UNICE Will Not Negotiate on National Information and Consultation', *European Industrial Relations Review* Vol. 291 (April), p. 3.

EIRR (1998c): 'Fixed-Term Contract Talks Begin', *European Industrial Relations Review*, Vol. 292 (May), p. 3.

EIRR (1998d): 'European Company Statute Nearing Adoption?' *European Industrial Relations Review*, Vol. 293 (June), pp. 24-27.

Ewing, Keith (ed.) (1996): *Working Life – A New Perspective on Labour Law*, London, Lawrence and Wishart.

Financial Times (1996): 'Brussels Riven by Job Market Row', London: *The Financial Times*, November 8, p. 2.

Fishback, Price, and Shawn Kantor (1995): 'Did Workers Pay for the Passage of Workers' Compensation Laws?', *Quarterly Journal of Economics*, Vol. 110 (August), pp. 713-42.

Gruber, Jonathan (1994): 'The Incidence of Mandated Maternity Benefits', *American Economic Review*, Vol. 84 (June), pp. 622-41.

Grubb, David, and William Wells (1993): 'Employment Regulation and Patterns of Work in EC Countries,' *OECD Economic Studies*, Vol. 21 (Winter), pp. 7-57.

Gyllenhammar (1998): *High Level Group on the Economic and Social Implications of Industrial Change, Interim Report*, Brussels, 14 May.

Hamermesh, Daniel S. (1989): 'The Demand for Workers and Hours and the Effects of Job Security Policies: Theories and Evidence', in Robert A. Hart (ed.), *Employment,*

Unemployment and Labor Utilization, Boston: Unwin-Hyman, pp. 9-32.

Hartog, Joop and Jules Theewes (1997): 'The Dutch Response To Dynamic Challenges in the Labour Market.' In Horst Siebert (ed.), *Structural Change and Labor Market Flexibility – Experience in Selected OECD Economies*, Tübingen: Mohr Siebeck, pp. 151-84.

Ichnowski, Casey, Karen Shaw, and Giovanna Prennushi (1997): 'The Effects of Human Resource Management Practices on Productivity: a Study of Steel Finishing Lines', *American Economic Review*, Vol. 87 (June 1997), pp. 291-313.

Kaestner, Robert (1996): 'The Effect of Government-Mandated Benefits on Youth Unemployment,' *Industrial and Labor Relations Review*, Vol. 50 (October), pp. 122-42.

Krueger, Alan R. (1994): 'Observations on Employment-Based Government Mandates, with Particular Reference to Health Insurance', in Lewis C. Solmon and Alec R. Stevenson (eds.), *Labor Markets, Employment Policy and Job Creation*, Boulder, San Francisco, and Oxford: Westview, pp. 197-326.

Krueger, Allan B. and Jörn-Steffen Pischke (1997): 'Observations and Conjectures on the US Employment Miracle', *Working Paper 6146*, National Bureau of Economic Research (August).

Layard, Richard, Stephen Nickell, and Richard Jackman (1991): *Unemployment*, Oxford: Oxford University Press.

Lazear, Edward P. (1990): 'Job Security Provisions and Employment,' *Quarterly Journal of Economics*, Vol. 105 (August), pp. 699-726.

Machin, S., A. Manning and S. Woodland (1993): 'Are Workers Paid Their Marginal Product? Evidence from a Low Wage Labour Market', *Discussion Paper 158*, Centre for Economic Performance, London School of Economics (July).

Martin, John. (1996): 'Measures of Replacement Rates for the Purposes of International Comparisons: A Note', *OECD Economic Studies*, Vol. 26, pp. 99-115.

Moore, Michael, and W. Kip Viscusi (1990): *Compensation Mechanisms for Job Risks: Wages, Workers' Compensation and Product Liability*, Princeton: Princeton University Press.

Morton, Jane, and W. Stanley Siebert (1997): 'Labour Regulation and Insider-Outsider Distinctions in the European Union', *Working Paper 976*, University of Birmingham, Department of Commerce (September).

Nickell, Stephen (1997): 'Unemployment and Labor Market Rigidities: Europe versus North America', *Journal of Economic Perspectives*, Vol. 11 (Summer), pp. 55-74.

Nickell, Stephen, and Brian Bell (1996): 'Changes in the Distribution of Wages and Unemployment in OECD Countries', *American Economic Review*, Vol. 86 (May), pp. 302-308.

OECD (1994): *Jobs Study, Part II*, Paris: Organisation for Economic Cooperation and Development.

OECD (1996): *Employment Outlook*, Paris: Organisation for Economic Cooperation and Development.

OECD (1997): *Employment Outlook*, Paris: Organisation for Economic Cooperation and Development.

Paqué, Karl-Heinz (1997): 'Does Europe's Common Market Need a "Social Dimension"? Some Academic Thoughts on a Popular Theme', in John T. Addison and W. Stanley Siebert (eds.), *Labour Markets in Europe – Issues of Harmonization and Regulation*, London and New York: The Dryden Press, pp. 105-17.

Saint-Paul, Giles (1997): *Dual Labor Markets: A Macroeconomic Perspective*, Massachusetts: MIT Press.

Scarpetta, Stefano (1996): 'Assessing the Role of Labour Market Policies and Institutional Settings on Unemployment: A Cross-Country Study,' *OECD Economic Studies*, Vol. 26, pp. 53-113.

Schmitter, Philippe C. (1977): 'Modes of Interest Intermediation and Models of Societal Change in Western Europe', *Comparative Political Studies*, Vol. 10, pp. 7-38.

Siebert, Horst (1997): 'Labor Market Rigidities: At the Root of Unemployment in Europe', *Journal of Economic Perspectives*, Vol. 11 (Summer), pp. 37-54.

Siebert, W. Stanley (1997): 'Overview of European Labour Markets', in John T. Addison and W. Stanley Siebert (eds.), *Labour Markets in Europe – Issues of Harmonization and Regulation*, London and New York: The Dryden Press, pp. 229-42.

Siebert, W. Stanley and Xiangdong Wei (1994): 'Compensating Wage Differentials for Workplace Accidents: Evidence from the 1983 General Household Survey for Union and Non-union Workers, *Journal of Risk and Uncertainty*, Vol. 9 (July), pp. 61-76.

Soltwedel, Rüdiger (1997): 'Social Engineering in Europe: A German Perspective', in John T. Addison and W. Stanley Siebert (eds.), *Labour Markets in Europe – Issues of Harmonization and Regulation*, London and New York: The Dryden Press, pp. 177-90.

Stevens, Margaret (1996): 'Transferable Training and Poaching Externalities', in Alison Booth and Dennis Snower (eds.), *Acquiring Skills*, Cambridge: Cambridge University Press, pp. 21-40.

Summers, Lawrence (1989): 'Some Simple Economics of Mandated Benefits', *American Economic Review*, Vol. 79 (May), pp. 177-83.

Teague, Paul (1989): *The European Community: The Social Dimension*, London: Kogan Page.

Williamson, Oliver, Michael Wachter, and Jeffrey Harris (1975): 'Understanding the Employment Relation: the Analysis of Idiosyncratic Exchange', *Bell Journal*, Vol. 6 (Spring), pp. 250-78.

Corporate Governance:

Accountability in the Marketplace

Elaine Sternberg

1. Businesses and corporations are not the same thing: not all corporations are businesses, and most businesses are not corporations. Whereas 'business' designates a particular objective, 'corporation' designates a particular organisational structure.

2. Corporate governance refers to ways of ensuring that corporate actions, assets and agents are directed at achieving the corporate objectives established by the corporation's shareholders (as set out in the Memorandum of Association or comparable constitutional document).

3. Many criticisms of corporate governance are based on false assumptions about what constitutes ethical conduct by corporations, and confusions about what corporate governance is.

4. Protests against takeovers, 'short-termism', redundancies and high executive remuneration are typically objections to specific corporate outcomes, not criticisms of corporate governance.

5. Many misguided criticisms of the Anglo-Saxon model come from confusing corporate governance with government: it is a mistake to criticise corporations for not achieving public policy objectives, and for not giving their stakeholders the rights and privileges commonly associated with citizenship.

6. Some criticisms of the traditional Anglo-Saxon model of corporate governance are justified. There are serious practical obstacles that prevent shareholders from keeping their corporations and corporate agents properly accountable.

7. Though commonly praised, the German and Japanese systems are considerably less capable of achieving the definitive purpose of corporate governance than the Anglo-Saxon model is. Neither is designed to protect, nor typically used for protecting, property rights.

8. The increasingly popular stakeholder theory is also incapable of providing better corporate governance. Stakeholder theory is incompatible with all substantial objectives and undermines both private property and accountability.

9. Regulation that attempts to improve corporate governance by limiting shareholders' options, and reducing their freedom to control their own companies as they choose, is necessarily counterproductive.

10. The way to respond to flaws in current Anglo-Saxon corporate governance mechanisms is to improve the accountability of corporations to their ultimate owners, preferably by having corporations compete for investment, and institutional investors for funds, in part on the degree of accountability they offer to their beneficial owners.

The Institute of Economic Affairs

2 Lord North Street, Westminster, London SW1P 3LB
Telephone: 0171 799 3745 Facsimile: 0171 799 2137
E-mail: iea@iea.org.uk Internet: http://www.iea.org.uk   ISBN 0-255 36416-4

£12.00

The Changing Fortunes of Economic Liberalism

Yesterday, Today and Tomorrow

David Henderson

1. Liberalism implies '...restricting the powers and functions of governments, so a to give full scope for individuals, families and enterprises.' But the state has an important role in '...establishing and maintaining a framework in which market can function effectively...'

2. The doctrine of economic liberalism goes back about two and a half centuries Over that period there has been no consistent trend towards liberal economic policies: indeed, liberalism was generally in decline over the hundred years up to the late 1970s.

3. But in the last two decades many governments have adopted reform programmes which have liberalised their economies and international transactions have been freed. The Economic Freedom of the World project, for example, shows a clear trend towards liberalisation in many countries - especially since 1985.

4. Few, if any, countries which have embarked on economic reform in the last twenty years have consciously reversed direction. The improvement in the fortunes of economic liberalism seems more than an 'accident of fashion'.

5. Reforming governments have appeared in every region of the world and from both the 'left' and the 'right' of the conventional political spectrum. They hav included authoritarian regimes though there is a strong association between political and economic freedoms.

6. It is not true that coalitions of interests largely preclude economic liberalisation otherwise, the reforms of recent years would not have taken place.

7. Liberal ideas have regained ground within the economics profession after a period from the 1930s to the 1970s when they were regarded as 'less central' than previously.

8. The 'balance of informed opinion' has also shifted to embrace liberal ideas. Politicians, civil servants and central bankers all came to support structural economic reforms from the mid-1980s onwards - even before the collapse of communism powerfully reinforced the liberal cause.

9. Despite the spread of liberal ideas, liberalism has a 'chronic weakness' becaus its conscious adherents are so few. In most countries majority opinion remain hostile to 'leaving it to the market', partly because of the continuing hold of pre-economic ideas.

10. Although events and continuing technical progress will probably continue to favour the liberal cause, anti-liberal ideas are still strong. Extending market reforms into areas so far untouched by liberalisation will be difficult. Hence the fortunes of economic liberalism in the early twenty first century are 'clouded and in doubt'.

The Institute of Economic Affairs

2 Lord North Street, Westminster, London SW1P 3LB
Telephone: 0171 799 3745 Facsimile: 0171 799 2137
E-mail: iea@iea.org.uk Internet: http://www.iea.org.uk

ISBN 0-255 36419-9

£12.00